CHILI

BREADS

TEX-MEX

MAIN DISHES

BARBECUE

SIDE DISHES

TEXAS

COOK BOOK

Tasty Texas Recipes and a side of Texas Trivia, too!

Edited by

Shayne K. Fischer

GOLDEN
WEST
PUBLISHERS

Texas trivia compiled by Al Fischer

Acknowledgments

We would like to gratefully express our thanks to: Adam's Extract, Amigos Canning Co., Brazos Country Foods, Carolyn Cole, Chef William Myers, John Billings, Imperial Sugar Company, Sam Overpeck, Mary Scott, Polly & Aubrey Smith, The Kingsford Company, *The Texas City Sun*, Texas Dept. of Agriculture, Texmati Rice, Tim Urquhart and all of the other helpful Texans who sent in their recipes. We appreciate your assistance in helping us prepare the ***Texas Cook Book!***

Printed in the United States of America

4th printing © 1996

ISBN # 0-914846-78-7

Golden West Publishers
4113 N. Longview Ave.
Phoenix, AZ 85014, USA
(602) 265-4392

Texas Information

State Seal: Five-pointed star enfolded by grain
State Motto: Friendship
Statehood: December 29, 1845 - the 28th state
State Bird: Mockingbird
State Tree: Pecan
State Flower: Bluebonnet
State Capital: Austin
State Nickname: Lone Star State
State Song: *"Texas, Our Texas"*
Area: Texas is second largest, after Alaska
Extent: Texas extends about 800 miles north-northwest to south-southeast, and about 750 miles east to west.
Population: Texas is now the third largest state in the nation with nearly 17 million persons, preceded only by California and New York.

Periods of Texas History

Indian Years	prior to 1519
Early Spanish Exploration	1519 to 1690
Mission Period and Spanish Colonization	1690-1793
Spanish Decline	1793-1821
Mexican Republic	1821-1836
Revolutionary Years	1835-1836
Republic of Texas	1836-1845
Early Statehood	1845
War with Mexico	1846-1848
Pre-Civil War	1848-1861
Texas in the Confederacy	1861-1865
Reconstruction and Early Development	1866-1899
Twentieth-Century Development	1900-1941
World War II to Twenty-First Century	1941-2000

Contents

APPETIZERS

BREAKFAST

SALADS

SOUPS

DESSERTS

BEVERAGES

Introduction

Texas is a big state and many of its features are on a grand scale. Texas offers a variety of climates and terrains—sunny seacoasts, mile-high mountains, teeming bayous, dense forests, cactus-studded deserts, and grassy plains.

Texas is big cities, vast ranches, huge farms, petroleum production and burgeoning high-tech industries. Texas is the Alamo, the Cowboys, the Oilers, the Rangers, the Astros. It is the home of NASA—the National Aeronautics and Space Administration.

Texas is great food. From the indigenous population to the coming of the Europeans and wave after wave of immigrants. Some food styles were imported from other parts of the United States along with the migrations from the South, the Midwest and the East. Other cuisines traveled with new Texans from the south; Texas is a vigorous variety of food styles.

Today's Texas-style foods, as featured in the ***Texas Cook Book***, include Tex-Mex, barbecue, Creole and Cajun, Asiatic and European of various ethnic sources. And, it makes use of such home-grown produce as chile peppers, black-eyed beans, grapefruit, pecans and peanuts, fish and shrimp from the gulf, beef from Texas-size herds and barbecued foods that use native mesquite for fuel and smoke.

To live in Texas is to celebrate life. Food festivals abound: chili cookoffs, shrimp harvests, barbecue contests, bed-and-breakfasts, Oktoberfests, Wurstfests, chuck-wagon cooking, local harvest events, fine restaurants and resorts.

Recipes included in the ***Texas Cook Book*** were submitted by executive chefs at famous Texas resorts, bed-and-breakfasts and restaurants. Others are from the collections of Texas homemakers, Texas food growers and manufacturers.

From Texas, the ***Texas Cook Book*** offers you appetizers, breakfasts, salads, soups, chili, breads, Tex-Mex, main dishes, barbecues, side dishes, desserts and beverages—enjoy them as the Texans do, wherever you live!

Creole Peanuts

Peanuts 3 cups, unsalted cocktail
Peanut oil 1/4 cup
Ranch style dressing mix 1 package
Dill weed 1 teaspoon, dried
Creole seasoning 1 teaspoon
Lemon pepper 1 teaspoon

Heat oil in small pan. Place peanuts in 13 x 9 x 2 pan. Pour warm oil over peanuts, stirring to coat. Mix last 4 ingredients together in small bowl. Pour over peanuts, stir well to coat. Bake in 350 degree oven for 12 minutes. Stir once while baking. Allow peanuts to cool before placing in airtight container.

Did You Know?

Texas is second in the nation in the production of peanuts. The annual crop is 682,500,000 pounds, valued at $191,100,000. The average annual per capita consumption of peanuts is 6.3 pounds.

Spiced Rubies

Grapefruit 5, Texas Ruby-Sweet or Rio Star
Sugar 2 cups
White vinegar 1 cup
Whole cloves 1 teaspoon
Cinnamon 2 sticks

Peel and section grapefruit over a bowl, reserving juice. Pack sections into jars and set aside.

Combine 1/2 cup grapefruit juice and remaining ingredients in a saucepan; bring to a boil, stirring constantly. Reduce heat and simmer 10 minutes. Strain to remove spices. Pour hot liquid into jars, covering sections completely. Cover and cool at room temperature. Refrigerate overnight before using. Makes about 3 half pints.

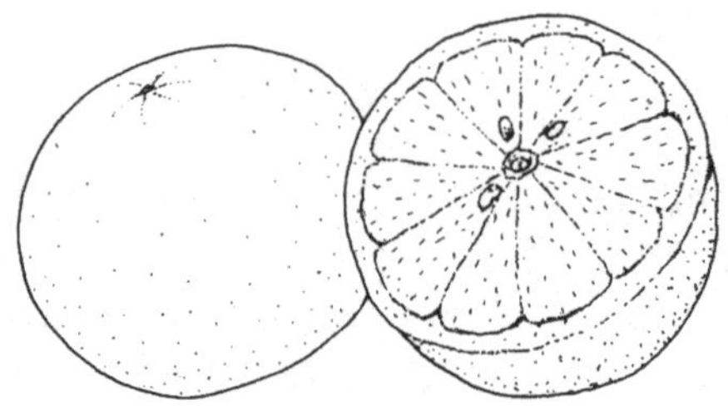

Texas grapefruit isn't just for breakfast any more. The sweet, juicy flavor and appetizing look of Rio Star and Ruby-Sweet grapefruit make this wholesome, nutritious food a natural for dishes ranging from salads to garnishes to desserts. What's more, grapefruit juice is a tasty addition to marinades and salad dressings.

Stuffed Garlic Bread

Tami Thomas - Texas City

Italian or French bread 1 large loaf, sliced lengthwise
Garlic 3 cloves, minced
Green olives 1 jar
Chives 1 bunch, trimmed
Jalapenos 3, seeded and chopped
Butter 1 cup
Miracle Whip® 1 cup
Cheese 3/4 cup, shredded jack
Cheese 3/4 cup, shredded cheddar

Combine garlic, olives, chives, jalapenos and butter in food processor. Process until smooth. Stir in dressing and cheese and spread on bread. Bake on cookie sheet at 350 degrees until bubbly and browned. Cut into 2-inch slices and serve hot. Serves about 18.

Almond Pine Cones

Billie Lambert - Santa Fe

Cream cheese 8-ounce package
Mayonnaise 1/2 cup
Bacon slices 5, cooked, drained, crumbled
Green onions 1 tablespoon, chopped
Dill weed 1/2 teaspoon
White pepper 1/8 teaspoon
Almonds 1 1/4 cups

Combine cream cheese and mayonnaise. Add bacon, green onions, dill and white pepper. Blend well and chill. Form into mound to look like 1/2 of a pine cone. Set aside.

Prepare almonds by spreading on a cookie sheet in a single layer. Bake at 300 degrees stirring often for 15 minutes or until barely brown. Cool almonds and decorate pine cone form in rows. Place small piece of parsley at top. Serve with your favorite crackers. Serves 4.

Sweet & Spicy Party Meatballs

Jerry Jares - Santa Fe

Cooking spray
Onion 1 large, minced
Ground beef 2 pounds, lean
Wheat germ 1/2 cup
Bread crumbs 3/4 cup, dried
Eggs 2
Chili powder 1/2 teaspoon
Seasoned salt 2 teaspoons
Black pepper 1/2 teaspoon
Chiles 4-ounce can, diced
Pineapple chunks 20-ounce can, in natural juice
Cornstarch 2 teaspoons
Apple jelly 8-ounce jar

Preheat oven to 350 degrees. Spray skillet with cooking spray. Add onions and sauté until tender. In a large bowl, combine the meat, wheat germ, bread crumbs, eggs, spices and chiles. Add the cooked onions.

Shape into 1-inch balls and place on jelly roll pan(s) to bake. After 15 minutes, take pans out of the oven and drain the grease. Return pans to oven for 15 more minutes. Drain and reserve 1/2 cup juice from pineapple. In a cup, stir reserved juice with cornstarch until smooth. Mix with jelly.

In a skillet, over medium heat, melt jelly mixture. Gradually stir in pineapple chunks, heat through.

Serve meatballs in chafing dish with toothpicks. Makes 3-4 dozen appetizers.

Note: Using jalapeno jelly instead of apple jelly is a wickedly delicious variation.

Stuffed Mushrooms

Nena Robinson - La Marque

Mushrooms 1 pound, large
Sausage 1 pound, bulk
Salt and pepper to taste
Garlic powder 1/4 teaspoon
Eggs 2
Parmesan cheese 1/4 cup, grated
Italian-style bread crumbs 3/4 cup
Olive oil 1/4 cup
Mozzarella cheese 1/2 cup, grated

Wash mushrooms and pat dry. Stem mushrooms and hollow caps slightly with spoon. Chop stems. Brown sausage and stems in a heavy skillet. Drain well. Remove from heat and cool. Add salt, pepper and garlic powder. Beat the eggs and parmesan cheese together and add to sausage mixture along with bread crumbs.

Mix well. Pour oil into a 13 x 9 x 2 inch baking dish and tilt to coat. Dip the outside of the mushroom caps in the oil and turn to coat. Stuff with sausage mixture and place side by side in baking dish. Sprinkle with mozzarella. Bake at 375 degrees for 20 minutes. Serve hot. Serves 4-6.

Vegetable Dip

Ola Marie Robison - Damon

Real mayonnaise 2 cups
Old English sharp cheese 2 small jars
Mustard 1 teaspoon
Worcestershire sauce 2 tablespoons
Tabasco® sauce dash
Garlic 1 clove, pressed

Mix with electric mixer and serve with a variety of fresh vegetables.

Holiday Chicken Patties

Erma Patterson - Texas City

Chicken or turkey 4 cups, finely chopped, cooked
Celery 1/2 cup, finely chopped
Onion 1/2 cup, finely chopped
Bread crumbs 1/4 cup, dry
Pimento 2-ounce jar, diced
Poultry seasoning 1/2 teaspoon
Salt and pepper to taste
Eggs 2, slightly beaten
Bread crumbs, additional (for coating)
Vegetable oil 2-4 tablespoons

Mix together all ingredients except eggs, additional bread crumbs and vegetable oil in medium bowl. Pour beaten eggs over chicken mixture and mix well. Chill. Shape into 8-10 patties. Coat each patty with bread crumbs. Heat oil in 10-inch skillet over medium heat until hot. Cook patties on each side until golden brown, about 10 minutes. Serve immediately. Serves 8-10.

Lumptuous Shrimp Dip

Carol Barclay - Portland

Shrimp 2 pounds, boiled, chopped
Cream cheese 24 ounces, softened
Celery 2 stalks
Green onions 6, tops and all
Jalapenos 2, large pickled
Jalapeno juice 1/2 teaspoon
Maraschino cherries 6
Mustard 1 tablespoon
Mayonnaise 1 small jar

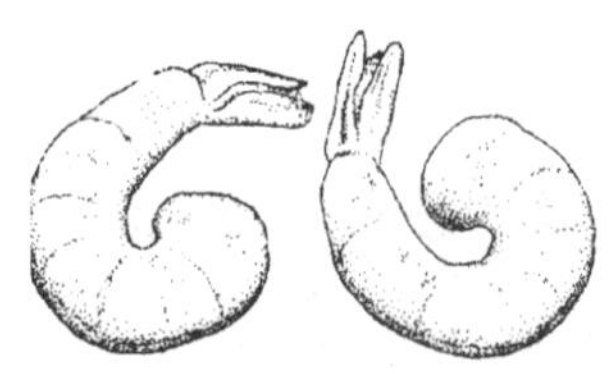

Mince celery, onions, jalapenos and cherries very small. Don't use blender or processor. Salt to taste. Add mustard and mayonnaise. Mix by hand and serve with chips or crackers. Without a doubt this is the best shrimp dip you will ever eat! Serves 10-12.

Almond Ring Appetizer

Jack Kivch - La Marque

Butter 1 stick
Salt 1/4 teaspoon
Ground pepper 1/4 teaspoon, fresh
Flour 1 cup, all-purpose
Eggs 4, whole
Gruyere cheese 1 1/2 cups (6 oz.), fresh grated
Nutmeg pinch of fresh grated
Egg yolk 1
Milk 1 tablespoon
Slivered almonds 1/2 to 3/4 cup

Preheat oven to 375 degrees. In heavy medium saucepan, combine butter, salt and pepper with 1 cup of water. Bring to a rolling boil over high heat. Remove from heat and add flour all at once. Using wooden spoon, beat until mixture is smooth and pulls away from sides of pan to form a ball. Continue to beat over low heat for 1 minute. Remove from heat and let cool for 1 minute. Beat in whole eggs, one at a time making sure each egg is completely incorporated before adding the next.

Stir in 1 1/4 cups of cheese and nutmeg. Mound large heaping spoonfuls of mixture on buttered baking sheet to form a wreath (inside edges measuring 7 inches across).

In small bowl, lightly beat egg yolk with milk. Using pastry brush, paint top of wreath with glaze. Sprinkle remaining 1/4 cup Gruyere and almonds over wreath. Bake almond ring 15 minutes, until puffed and set. Reduce heat to 350 degrees and cook for 45 minutes longer, until golden brown and firm to touch. Let cool for 10 minutes and serve warm. Serves 8-10.

Bacon Cheese Ball

Lela Giles - Texas City

Cream cheese 2 (8 oz.) packages, softened
Mayonnaise 1/2 cup
Salad dressing mix 4-ounce package, buttermilk style
Green onions 1/4 cup, chopped
Bacon 10 slices, cooked and crumbled
Green onion fan 1
Bacon curl 1, crisp
Crackers

Beat cream cheese until smooth. Blend in mayonnaise. Stir in salad dressing mix, chopped green onions and crumbled bacon. Cover and chill at least 3 hours. Shape into a ball. Garnish with green onion fan and bacon curl. Serve with crackers.

Christmas Dip

Bonnie Dixon - Alvarado

Flour 1 tablespoon
Sugar 1 tablespoon
Salt 1 teaspoon
Vinegar 4 tablespoons
Butter or margarine 2 tablespoons
Egg yolks 2, beaten
Cream cheese 8-ounce package, softened
Bell pepper 1 small, chopped
Onion 1 small, chopped
Pimentos 1 small jar, drained
chop and set aside

In double boiler add flour, sugar, salt, vinegar and butter. When this has melted and mixed, add the two beaten egg yolks. Stir and then add this to cream cheese and chopped bell pepper, onion and pimentos. Stir all together and refrigerate.

"Tomball Texas"–Crabmeat Hors D'oeuvres

Ola Marie Robison - Damon

Crabmeat 8-ounce can, drained and flaked
Onion 2-3 tablespoons, finely chopped
Celery 2-3 tablespoons, finely chopped
Worcestershire sauce 1 teaspoon
Salad dressing or sour cream to moisten
Triscuit® crackers
Grated cheese

Combine first five ingredients. Place one teaspoon on each cracker. Sprinkle with grated cheese. Broil until toasted.

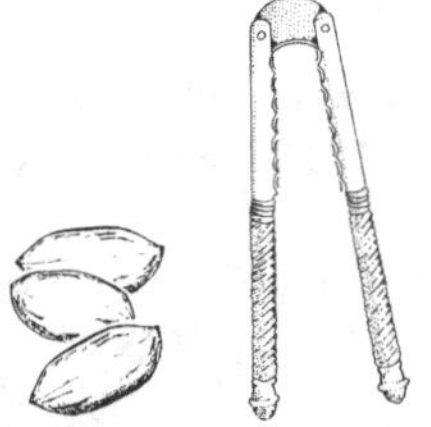

Doris's Orange Pecans

Texas Pecan Growers Association - College Station

Orange 1
Sugar 1 cup
Pecan halves 2 cups
Wax paper

Scrape zest (rind) from orange. Juice orange and mix with zest and sugar. Bring to boil over medium heat stirring constantly. Add pecans and continue boiling over fairly high heat, stirring vigorously until most of the juice has been absorbed (about 5 minutes). Spread quickly on wax paper to cool, separating pecans with a fork.

Rice 'n Cheese Spread

Texmati Brands Rice Products - Alvin

Texmati® Rice 1 cup, cooked
Cheddar cheese 1/2 pound, grated
Onion 1/2 tablespoon, minced
Green pepper 3 tablespoons, minced
Olives 3, stuffed chopped
Pickle relish 3 tablespoons
Pimento 1 tablespoon, chopped
Egg 1, hard cooked, chopped
Saltine crackers 1/2 cup, finely chopped
Mayonnaise 1/4 cup
Salt 1/2 teaspoon

Combine first 7 ingredients. Add remaining ingredients, mixing well. Shape into a long roll. Serve with assorted crackers.

Wonton Oysters

Carol Barclay - Portland

Wonton wraps
Oysters
Cream cheese softened
Garlic salt
Vegetable oil for frying

Quarter oysters. On each wonton wrap place a piece of oyster; top with small piece of cream cheese. Sprinkle with garlic salt. Gather wonton dough ends together to seal edges; drop into hot cooking oil (325 degrees) and cook until golden brown.

Seguin is famous as the "Home of the World's Largest Pecan." This oversized "nut," made of metal and plastic, a monument to the state tree of Texas, is displayed at courthouse square in the middle of town.

Orange/Pecan McKay House Toast

McKay House - Dallas

Eggs 4
Orange juice 2/3 cup
Milk 1/3 cup
Sugar 1/4 cup
Nutmeg 1/4 teaspoon, ground
Vanilla extract 1/2 teaspoon
Orange liqueur 1/4 cup
Orange zest 1 tablespoon
Italian or French bread 8-ounce loaf, cut in 1-inch thick slices
Butter or margarine 1/3 cup, melted
Pecan pieces 1/2 cup

With wire whisk beat together eggs, orange juice, milk, sugar, nutmeg, vanilla, orange zest and orange liqueur. Place bread in single layer in tight-fitting casserole. Pour milk mixture over bread. Cover and refrigerate overnight, turning once. Preheat oven to 400 degrees. Pour melted butter on a jelly roll pan, spreading evenly. Arrange soaked bread slices in a single layer on pan. Sprinkle with pecans. Bake until golden, 20 to 25 minutes.

As option, may place under broiler for 1-2 minutes to give a toasty appearance, sprinkle with powdered sugar. Remove from pan onto garnished plate and serve immediately. Serve with maple syrup and butter or with fresh fruit. Serves 4.

Scrambled Eggs with Jalapeno Cheese

Helen K. Taylor - Riverview Farm

Eggs 6
Water 1 teaspoon
Milk 1 teaspoon
Jalapeno cheese 8 ounces, 1" cubes
(Monterrey with jalapenos)

Mix all of above well. Pour into lightly oiled skillet and scramble to desired consistency, preferably moist. Serves 4.

Brook House Mexi-Cheese Grits

The Brook House Bed & Breakfast - Austin

Grits 2 cups instant
Water 8 cups
Salt 2 teaspoons
Butter 1 cup
Cheese 1 1/2 pounds (3 cups) Colby-Jack
Salt 2 1/2 teaspoons, seasoned
Worcestershire sauce 1 1/2 teaspoon
Eggs 8, beaten slightly
Tomatoes 1 can rotel, drained
Green chiles 1 (4 oz.) can, chopped
(Garlic chives and paprika to garnish)

Boil water and salt, add grits, cook 2-5 minutes. Add butter and cheese, stir until melted. Add seasoned salt and Worcestershire. Fold in eggs, tomatoes and chiles. Pour into greased 9 x 13 baking pan. Bake 1 hour at 350 degrees. Allow 10-15 minutes to cool and "set up" before serving. Serves 15-18.

Breakfast Tacos

Carol Barclay - Portland

Sausage 1 pound, hot
Hash brown potatoes 2-pound bag, frozen
Green bell pepper 1, chopped
Red bell pepper 1, chopped
Onion 1, chopped
Celery ribs 3, finely chopped
Eggs 6, beaten
Cheddar cheese 1 pound, grated
Flour tortillas
Picante sauce

Brown sausage in frying pan; drain. Add hash browns, peppers, onion, celery and eggs. Mix. Butter a 9 x 13 casserole or spray with non-stick spray. Place taco mixture in casserole and bake at 350 degrees for 45 minutes. Top with cheese and heat until melted. To serve, place a large scoop of potato mixture on a warmed tortilla, add picante sauce if desired, roll up and enjoy. Serves 4-6.

Rancher's Omelet

Carmen Dougherty - Marion

Bacon 6 slices, diced
Onion 2 tablespoons, finely chopped
Potatoes 1 cup, grated raw
Eggs 6, slightly beaten
Salt 1/2 teaspoon
Black pepper 1/8 teaspoon
Hot sauce dash
Parsley 2 tablespoons, minced

Fry bacon until crisp, drain all but 2 tablespoons drippings, add potatoes and onions and cook until light brown. Pour eggs into skillet, add salt, pepper and hot sauce. Lift up edges with spatula to let uncooked egg mixture slide underneath. When firm, sprinkle with bacon and parsley. Fold omelet in half. Serve immediately.

Texas Eggs Poupon

Patricia Ann Roberts - Midland

Egg yolks 12, mashed from 1 dozen hard boiled eggs
Egg white halves 24, hard boiled
Grey Poupon Dijon® mustard 1/3 cup
Pimentos 2 ounces, chopped
Parsley 2 small sprigs, fresh

Boil 1 dozen eggs until hard cooked. Cool and peel. Slice lengthwise and remove yolks, putting them in small mixing bowl. Mash until all lumps are smooth. Stir mustard and pimentos into egg yolks and mix thoroughly. Add more mustard if mixture is dry. Spoon mixture into egg whites and arrange on egg plate. Serve chilled with sprigs of parsley. 24 servings.

Note: No-cholesterol eggs may be used in place of yolks.

Tips: Serve on egg plate; if not available, use any round plate for eye appeal. Chill with plastic wrap to prevent dryness. Do not consume any leftovers after 48 hours of refrigeration.

Texas Flapjacks

Mary Beth Drain - Denton

Flour 2 cups
Baking powder 1 tablespoon
Salt 1 teaspoon
Milk 1 cup
Vegetable oil or shortening 1 cup

Mix all dry ingredients thoroughly. Add milk to mixture until the dough is thick. Set aside. Pour oil or shortening in skillet and preheat. Drop the dough from a tablespoon into hot oil or shortening. Cook until golden brown. Serves 6.

Grapefruit Crunch

Grapefruit sections Texas Ruby-Sweet or Rio Star, drained
Yogurt 1 tablespoon, pina colada-flavored low-fat
Granola 1 tablespoon

Arrange grapefruit sections in a shallow bowl. Top with yogurt. Sprinkle with granola. Serves 1.

Mild winters with plenty of sunshine are generally found at Utopia on the River, a bed-and-breakfast resort near Utopia, west of San Antonio. Summer days here are great for floating down the river, spring is fine for fishing, hiking and bird-watching, and winter is the season for deer and turkey hunting.

Rum Runner Blueberry Pancakes

Utopia on the River - Utopia

Buttermilk Pancake Mix 3 1/2 cups
Water 1 1/2 cups
Club soda 1 cup
Rum 1 jigger
Whole blueberries 3/4 cup, frozen or fresh

Preheat griddle to 375-400 degrees. Mix pancake mix, water, club soda and rum. Mix well, but do not overheat. Stir in blueberries and bake on preheated griddle. Flip when edges begin to dry, approximately 1 1/2 minutes. Flip only once. Bake for 1 1/4 to 1 1/2 minutes on second side. Serves 12-16.

Holiday House Salad

Linda Crisp - Dickinson

Potatoes 2 1/2 pounds, cooked, diced
Mayonnaise 1/2 cup
Deviled ham 3-ounce can
Milk 1 tablespoon
Onion 3 tablespoons, chopped
Salt 1/2 teaspoon
Pepper 1/8 teaspoon
Celery salt 1/8 teaspoon
Parsley chopped
Parsley sprigs
Green pepper strips
Carrot 1

Combine potatoes, mayonnaise, ham, milk, onion and seasonings. Blend well and chill. Using 2/3 of potato salad mixture press into a solid square or rectangle on a bread board or tray. This forms the house itself.

Using remaining potato salad, press into a sloped roof on top of house. Sprinkle roof with chopped parsley and insert a square piece of carrot for chimney. Fashion door and windows with green pepper strips. Thin carrot strips on either side of windows serve as shutters. Garnish sides of house with parsley sprigs for shrubbery. Serves 6.

Grapefruit and Avocado Salad

Grapefruit 2 Ruby Red
Avocados 2, peeled and sliced
Purple onion 1 small, sliced
Salad greens 4 cups, torn into pieces

Peel, seed and section grapefruit. Combine with avocado slices, onion and salad greens.

Toss gently with the following dressing. Refrigerate for 1/2 hour before serving.

Dressing:
Sugar 1/2 cup
Dry mustard 1/2 teaspoon
Salt 3/4 teaspoon
Vinegar 1/4 cup
Vegetable oil 3/4 cup
Poppy seeds 1 1/2 tablespoons

Beat all ingredients together until thoroughly mixed. Keep refrigerated.

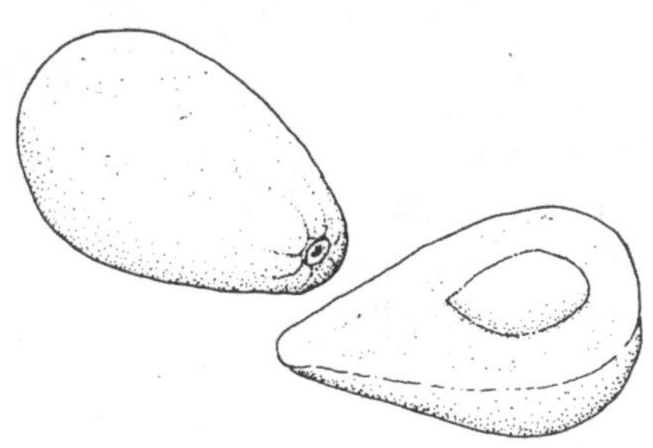

Texas has built its grapefruit industry on production of pink and red varieties. In 1929, the Ruby Red fruit was discovered growing on a pink grapefruit tree in the lower Rio Grande valley. Today, it constitutes 95 percent of the grapefruit grown in Texas groves and is shipped throughout the world.

Shrimp Salad

Texas City Sun

Shrimp 2 pounds boiled, peeled and cleaned
Onion 1/2 medium, diced
Bell pepper 1/2 medium, diced
Celery 1 stalk, diced
Sweet pickle relish 2 tablespoons
Eggs 2, hard boiled, diced
Mayonnaise 3 tablespoons
Salt and pepper to taste

In mixing bowl, put diced shrimp and all other ingredients and mix. Place in covered casserole dish and chill. Serve with saltine crackers. Serves 6-8.

Heavenly Holiday Fruit Salad

Texas City Sun

Mixed fruit 2 cans, well drained
Mandarin oranges 1 small can, well drained
Apple 1 small red, cored and chopped
Green apple 1 small, cored and chopped
Bananas 2 medium, sliced
Sweetened coconut 1 cup, shredded
Walnuts or pecans 3/4 cup, chopped
Cool Whip® 8-ounce container
Mini-marshmallows 1/2 package, colored, fruit flavored

Combine all ingredients in a large bowl, mixing gently but well. Chill well at least one hour or until ready to serve. Serves a small army.

Texas City is a city of about 45,000 on Galveston Bay between Houston and Galveston, Texas. It was incorporated in 1911, but its history goes back to the 1800's, when farmers and ranchers settled near Shoal Point, a spit of land marked by a lighthouse.

Zesty Bean Salad

Jerry Jares - Santa Fe

Beans 3 cans of different (pinto, northern, navy, kidney, ranch-style, butter beans, red), drained and rinsed
Green onions 4, thinly chopped
Red or green pepper 1, seeded and finely chopped
Chopped parsley
Olive oil 3 tablespoons
Cider vinegar 2 tablespoons
Garlic clove 1, minced
Dry mustard 1/8 teaspoon
Pepper

Select three bean types that offer colorful contrast. Drain and rinse each; pour into a bowl. Add onions, red pepper and parsley. To make the dressing, add the olive oil and remaining ingredients into a jar and shake well. Pour dressing over the bean salad. Marinade in refrigerator for 1 hour. Adjust seasonings and serve. Makes 8 generous servings.

Fresh Corn Salad

Erma Patterson - Texas City

Corn 5 medium ears
Celery 1 1/2 cups, chopped
Green pepper 1/2 cup, chopped
Eggs 3 hard cooked, chopped
Pimento 2 tablespoons, diced
Mayonnaise 1/2 cup
Onion 1 teaspoon, grated
Lemon juice 2 teaspoons, fresh
Sugar 1 teaspoon
Salt 1 1/2 teaspoon, optional
Pepper 1/8 teaspoon
Hot pepper sauce dash

Boil corn, cool and cut from cob. Mix with celery, green pepper, eggs and pimento. Combine remaining ingredients. Stir into corn mixture. Chill. Serves 6.

Beet Dessert/Salad

Jack Kivch - La Marque

Pineapple 16-ounce can, crushed, with the juice
Beets 8-ounce can, diced in small pieces
Apple cider vinegar 2 tablespoons
Lemon juice 8 tablespoons, fresh
Jello® 6-ounce package or 2 (3 oz.) packages, raspberry
Pecans 1 cup, toasted, chopped

Drain off the juice from the pineapple and the beets. Place in sauce pan and add 2 tablespoons apple cider vinegar and the lemon juice. With the juices included, add enough water to make 3 1/4 cups liquid. Bring to a rolling boil. Remove from heat and add to the jello in a large bowl. Let set until partially congealed. Add the crushed pineapple, diced beets and chopped nuts. Chill until firm. Serves 6-8.

Optional: Top with whipped cream or Cool Whip® and chopped toasted pecans.

Artichoke-Mushroom Toss

Lela Giles - Texas City

Italian salad dressing mix 1-ounce package
Salad seasonings 1 teaspoon
Artichoke hearts 14-ounce can, drained
Olives 3/4 cup, pitted ripe
Water chestnuts 8-ounce can, drained
Mushrooms 8-ounce package, fresh, sliced
Leaf lettuce 1 large head, torn into bite-size pieces
Spinach 1/2 pound, torn into bite-size pieces

Prepare salad dressing mix as directed on package. In large snap and seal plastic bag, combine Italian dressing, salad seasonings, artichokes, olives, water chestnuts and mushrooms. Chill up to 24 hours. Just before serving, add greens to marinated mixture. Close tightly and shake to coat. Pour into bowl.

Corn, Bean and Rice Salad

Lee Lambert - Santa Fe

Converted rice 3 1/2 cups, cooked, cooled
Pink beans 16 oz. can, rinsed and drained (can use pinto beans)
Corn kernels 1 1/2 cups, cooked, fresh or 12-ounce can
Scallions 1/3 cup, chopped
Jalapeno peppers 2, pickled, stemmed, seeded, de-ribbed and minced
Safflower or corn oil 1/3 cup
Lime juice 2 tablespoons, fresh
Cider vinegar 1 tablespoon
Brown sugar 1 tablespoon, packed
Chili powder 1 teaspoon
Salt 1 teaspoon
Ground cumin 1/2 teaspoon

In large bowl, combine the rice, beans, corn, scallions and jalapeno peppers. Toss to mix.

In a small bowl, combine the oil, lime juice, vinegar, brown sugar, chili powder, salt and cumin. Whisk until sugar dissolves and mixture well-blended. Pour the dressing over the salad and toss to coat.

Let stand at room temperature, tossing occasionally, for up to 4 hours or cover and refrigerate up to 3 days. Serves 6-8.

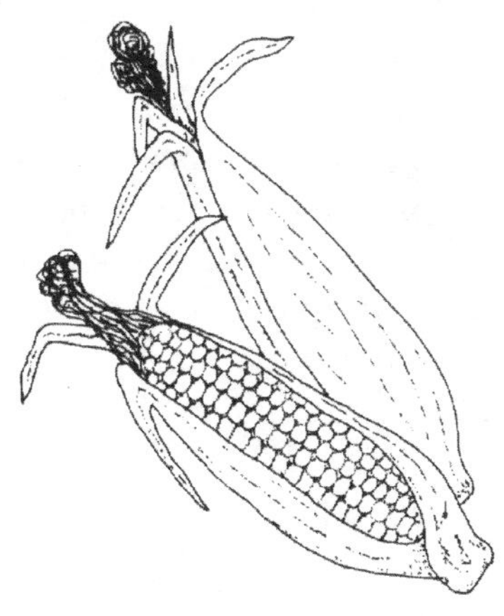

Fruit Toss w/Orange Pecan Dressing

Norton Brackenridge House - San Antonio

Fruit:

Honeydew melon 1 medium, seeded, cut into 1" pieces
Strawberries 1 pint (2 cups), fresh halved
Blueberries 1 pint (2 cups), fresh

Dressing:

Dairy sour cream 1 cup
Powdered sugar 1/4 cup
Orange juice 1/4 cup
Pecans 1/3 cup finely chopped

In large salad bowl, combine fruits, toss gently. In small bowl, combine sour cream, powdered sugar and orange juice; blend well. Stir in pecans. Refrigerate fruit and dressing until serving time. Serve dressing with fruit.

The Norton-Brackenridge House, a lovely, restored bed-and-breakfast home near downtown San Antonio, is a two-story Greek Revival home built in 1906 and restored on its 80th birthday. Filled with antiques and plants, the home gets its comfortable ambiance from the numerous family heirlooms and memorabilia. Guests select from four downstairs bedrooms, each with a private entrance, private bath and queen-sized bed.

Delicious Fruit Salad

Louise Porter - Big Spring

Pineapple tidbits 1 cup
Apples 1 cup, chopped
Peaches 1 cup, canned or fresh
Strawberries 2 cups, whole
Bananas 1 cup, sliced
Coconut 1 cup, flaked
Lemon juice
Low-fat yogurt

Mix all fruit carefully. Sprinkle a little lemon juice over the fruit. Use enough low-fat yogurt, any fruit flavor, to mix with and cover the fruit. This salad will keep several days refrigerated and tastes better all the time.

Avocado and Banana Salad

Mary Emma Wagnon - Seguin

Avocados 2
Bananas 4 medium or 3 large
Lemon or lime juice 3 tablespoons, freshly squeezed
Sugar 2 tablespoons
Mayonnaise 1/2 cup

Dice avocado. Mix with sliced bananas. Add lemon or lime juice and stir to coat to prevent discoloration. Add sugar and allow to stand until dissolved. Mix in mayonnaise. Chill before serving. Serves 6.

Tip: Good served with chicken or tuna salad.

Broccoli & Macaroni Salad

Beverly McClatchy - Midland

Macaroni 1 package, curly
Broccoli 1 cup fresh flowerets
Black olives small can, sliced
Green olives sliced
Pimento small jar
Green onion tops chopped
Italian dressing 1 bottle

Cook and cool macaroni as directed on package. Mix remaining ingredients and add macaroni. Chill. Serves 12.

Tip: This salad is good the next day if stored in a tight container.

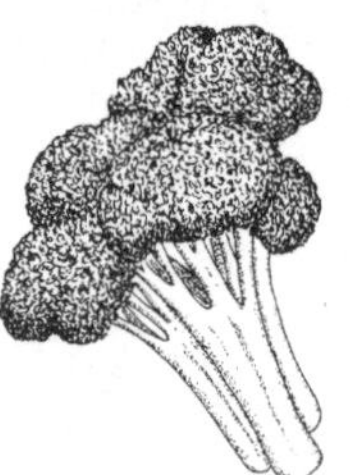

Cauliflower & Broccoli Salad

Beverly McClatchy - Midland

Broccoli flowerets large bunch
Cauliflower large head
Green olives sliced
Green onion chopped

Dressing:
Buttermilk salad dressing mix 1 package
Miracle Whip® 3/4 cup
Sugar 2 tablespoons
Vinegar 2 tablespoons

Mix broccoli, cauliflower, olives and onion. In small bowl mix salad dressing mix, Miracle Whip, sugar and vinegar. Pour over vegetables and mix well. Refrigerate. Serves 8.

Layered Turkey & Rice Salad

Texmati Brand Rice Products - Alvin

Turkey 2 cups cooked and chopped
Lettuce 2 cups torn
Texmati® rice 2 cups cooked
Peas 1 (10 oz.) package frozen
Parsley 1/2 cup chopped
Water chestnuts 1 can
Tomato 1 large chopped
Red bell pepper 1 small chopped
Green bell pepper 1 small chopped

Layer 1/2 the turkey and lettuce in a large bowl. Combine rice, peas and parsley. Spoon 1/2 over turkey and lettuce. Layer remaining ingredients. Add remaining rice mixture, then remaining turkey and lettuce. Top with dressing (below) sealing to the edge of the bowl. Cover and chill 8 hours.

Dressing:
Mayonnaise 2 cups
Sour cream 1 cup
Onion 1/2 cup finely chopped
Sweet pickle relish 1/2 cup
Garlic salt 1/2 teaspoon
Milk 4 tablespoons
Celery seed 1 teaspoon
Dill seed 1 teaspoon
Dry mustard 1 teaspoon

Combine all ingredients mixing well.

San Antonio Bean Soup

Dried beans 1 pound mixture of your favorite
Hambone 1
Water 2 quarts
Salt, pepper and garlic powder to taste
Onion 1 medium, coarsely chopped
Celery 2 stalks, chopped
Carrots 2, chopped
Bell pepper 1 small, chopped
Ham 2 cups, diced

Soak beans overnight. In the morning, drain water and put beans in a large soup pot. Add hambone, 2 quarts water and seasonings. Simmer 2-3 hours. Add vegetables and ham, and more water if needed. Simmer until vegetables are tender.

San Antonio, one of America's most colorful cities, exudes old Spanish charm. The site was a Coahuitecan Indian village when a Franciscan mission, San Antoni de Valero and its protecting fort, were built in 1718. The mission was later renamed "The Alamo" from the Spanish word for cottonwood tree.

Houston Hearty Bean Soup

Ground beef 1/2 pound, lean
Onion 1, chopped
Kidney beans 15-ounce can
Corn 8-ounce can
Tomatoes 14-ounce can, chopped
Tomato sauce 8-ounce can
Chili powder 2 teaspoons
Garlic powder 1/4 teaspoon
Water 1 1/2 cups

Brown ground beef with onion. Stir in remaining ingredients. Simmer for 30 minutes. Serves 6-8.

Houston, Texas' largest city, is also the fourth largest city in the nation. Although it's fifty miles from the Gulf of Mexico, it's one of the country's major seaports due to the conversion of the marshy Buffalo Bayou into the Houston Ship Canal. Cotton, cattle and timber shipping made it a thriving city, but its economy boomed due to the discovery of petroleum.

Creamy Cauliflower Soup

Onion 1 medium, chopped
Flour 3 tablespoons
Margarine 3 tablespoons
Chicken bouillon 3 cubes
Water 3 cups
Cauliflower 2 cups, frozen or fresh
Milk or cream 1 1/2 cups
Grated cheese 1 cup
Salt and pepper to taste

Sauté onion in flour and margarine. Add bouillon cubes, water and cauliflower. Cook over low heat until cauliflower is tender. Add milk and heat through. Stir in cheese until melted. Season to taste. Serves 6.

Corn Chowder

Bacon 1/2 pound
Onion 1, chopped
Green bell pepper 1, chopped
Potatoes 1 cup, cubed
Water 1 cup
Corn 1 1/2 cups, cut from 3 ears
Milk 2 cups
Butter 3 tablespoons
Salt and pepper to taste

In a kettle, fry bacon, reserving enough fat to sauté onion, bell pepper and potatoes. When onion is translucent, add water and bring to a boil. Cut corn from cob. Add corn, milk, butter and seasonings. Lower flame and simmer until corn is tender (approximately 10 minutes). Serve hot. Serves 4-6.

The first word uttered on the moon in July 1969 was "Houston." American astronauts were checking in with NASA's Lyndon B. Johnson Space Center.

Black-eyed Peas

Black-eyed peas 1 pound, dried
Water 6 cups
Onion 1/2 cup, chopped
Salt and pepper to taste
Bacon 8 strips, cut up or 1/2 pound diced ham
Butter or margarine 1 stick

Place dried peas in a pot with water and soak overnight. Add onion, salt, pepper, bacon or diced ham. Bring mixture to a slow boil. Turn down heat and simmer for 1 hour. Add water if necessary. When peas are tender, add butter, and check for seasoning. Add more salt and pepper if needed. Serves 8.

Bramborova Polivka (Potato Soup)

Lebbie Fravnicek Dirks - Big Spring

Water 2 quarts
Potatoes 6 medium
Margarine 4 tablespoons
Onion 1 medium-large
Flour 2-3 tablespoons
Egg 1
Salt and pepper to taste

Peel and cut potatoes in bite-sized chunks. Boil in extra amount of salted water till soft. Save all water. When potatoes are nearly done, melt margarine in skillet, add diced onion and flour. Sauté until golden brown. Then add some of the potato water and cook for 2 minutes or so. Pour into kettle with rest of potatoes and water. Mix well and heat thoroughly. Beat egg with a fork and add slowly to the soup, stirring constantly. Cook until egg is done. Serves 6.

Tip: "May add crumbled bacon or rice. So good that Texans love it! We used to call this 'Poor Man's Soup' when we were children. It is most filling."

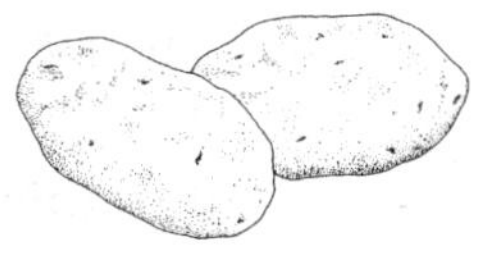

Poblano Chili Soup

Larry Eason - Texas City

Onion 1/4 cup, grated
Chicken stock 2 cups, canned or homemade
Green chiles 4-ounce can, chopped
Cream cheese 8-ounce package
Yogurt 8-ounce container, plain
Lime 4 thin slices, fresh
Cilantro 2 tablespoons, for garnish

Simmer grated onion in the chicken stock 10 minutes. Remove from heat. Add the chiles, cream cheese and yogurt. Process in processor or puree in blender in small batches. To serve hot, reheat at low temperature or serve cold. Add a slice of lime and a garnish of cilantro to each bowl. Serves 4.

Cheese Vegetable Soup

Wild Briar - The Country Inn at Edom - Ben Wheeler

Carrot 1/2 cup finely chopped
Onion 1/4 cup finely chopped
Potato 1/2 cup chopped
Celery 1/4 cup finely chopped
Green pepper 1/4 cup finely chopped
Tomato 1/4 cup finely chopped, without seeds
Flour 1/4 cup
Salt and pepper 1/2 teaspoon each
Sugar 1/4 cup
Water 1/2 cup
American cheese 1 cup, chopped
Chicken broth 1 can
Milk 2 cups

Cover all of the vegetables in water and microwave for ten minutes. Mix flour, salt, pepper and sugar with water in a sauce pan. Stir until thick. Add cheese and when melted add chicken broth to mixture. Add milk and cooked vegetables.

"At Wild Briar, we put milk and broth in our crockpot, add cooked cheese and flour mixture, add vegetables and simmer until ready to serve. If you use skim milk, it will not be smooth, but the taste will be the same. We use whole milk or canned milk. Heat serving bowls before adding soup."

An east Texas country inn, the Wild Briar, located in Edom, is a combination of British-Welsh-Scottish-French and Texan charm. The owners, after having toured the British Isles for five years, decided to build their own country inn. The home, constructed of moss-colored brick, has six guest bedrooms and offers breakfast, dinner, and lodging.

Chili was probably invented by chuckwagon cooks of southwestern Texas accustomed to preparing their own brand of stew for cowboys out on the range. Possibly, one of these cooks ran out of the customary black pepper. In his search for a substitute, he came across some red peppers commonly in vogue among the Indians or Mexicans in the area. When the cowboys complained of the intensity of the red pepper stew, they were advised that the heat of the dish was generated by the "chile," a generic term that refers to hot peppers. As time passed, the searing stew was acknowledged as an entity in its own right, and "chili" was born.

Abilene Texas Chili

Bacon grease 4 tablespoons
Onions 2 large, chopped
Garlic 6 cloves, chopped
Salt to taste
Ground beef 2 pounds
Chili powder 3 tablespoons
Tomatoes 2 (20 oz.) cans
Kidney beans 20 ounce can, red
Comino seeds 2 tablespoons, tied in a bag

Heat bacon grease in skillet. Add onions and garlic and cook until tender, but not brown. Mix meat with salt and chili powder and add to onions. Cook until meat is done. Add tomatoes, beans and comino seed. Simmer covered for about 2 hours. Makes 2 quarts.

Venison Chili

The Mansion on Turtle Creek - Dallas

Pasilla chiles 4, seeded and stems removed
Ancho chiles 4, seeded and stems removed
Chile de arbol 1, seeded and stem removed
Chicken stock 1 1/2 cups, more if needed
Corn tortillas 3, quartered
Corn or other light oil 5 tablespoons
Venison stew meat 2 pounds, cut not ground into 1/2 inch cubes
Yellow onions 1 large or 2 small, peeled and minced
Garlic 6 cloves, peeled and minced
Ground cumin 3 tablespoons
Dark beer 16 ounces
Venison, beef or chicken stock 1 quart
Cinnamon stick 1
Fresh cilantro 10 sprigs, tied in a bundle
Limes 2, juiced
Salt and pepper to taste

Combine chiles and 1 1/2 cups chicken stock in a medium sauce pan over high heat. Bring to a boil, then lower heat and simmer for 10 minutes stirring twice, or until chiles are soft. Cool slightly. Pour into a blender. Add tortillas and puree until smooth. Chili mixture should be quite thick, with just enough liquid to puree. Add more stock if necessary.

Heat oil in a large sauté pan over medium-high heat. When oil smokes, add venison cubes and cook, stirring frequently, until browned. Season with salt and pepper. Remove meat with a slotted spoon and set aside.

While oil is still hot, stir in onion and cook for 5 minutes or until well browned. Add garlic and cumin and cook for 1 minute. Add chili puree and fry for about 7 minutes or until thick and very dark, stirring often to keep from scorching.

When thick, add meat, beer and 4 cups chicken stock, stirring well. Lower heat and simmer, uncovered, for 1 hour or until very thick and reduced by half. Remove from heat and stir in the cinnamon and cilantro bundle. Let stand, without stirring, for 15 minutes. Remove cinnamon and cilantro and stir in lime juice. Season with salt and pepper. Serves 4.

Corral Chili

Virginia Gentry - Midland

Lean ground meat 5 pounds
Salt 3 teaspoons
Vegetable oil 2 tablespoons
Morton's® Chili Blend 1 cup
Onion powder 1 tablespoon
Garlic powder 1 tablespoon
Red chile peppers 7 large, dry
Comino seed 2 teaspoons
Tomato sauce 2 (15 oz.) cans
Pumpkin 1 (15 oz.) can

Use a 6 quart pressure sauce pan. Brown meat in the oil, add salt. Cover meat with water. Add Chili Blend, onion powder, garlic powder, peppers and comino seed and mix well. Pressure 30 minutes at 15 pounds pressure. When pressure goes down, add tomato sauce and pumpkin, simmer 15-20 minutes. Remove chili peppers before serving. Serves 8-16.

Tip: Serve hot with crackers, ketchup or cheese cubes. Makes a good sauce for a chili dog. Freezes well.

Easy Chili

Pat Stone - Conroe

Chili 1 large can, with beans
Chili beans 1 (33 oz.) can
Vacuum-packed whole kernel corn 1 small can
Cheddar cheese 1 cup grated
Onion 1 small, finely chopped
Green chile pepper 1 small, finely chopped
Corn chips 1 bag, broken

Combine all ingredients except chips and cook in crock pot until cheese is melted and ingredients are bubbling. Add bag of chips and continue to cook until bubbling again. Ready to serve. Serves 10-12.

Fiery Pot Texas Chili

Imperial Sugar Company - Sugar Land

Someone in the know once said, "There are only two people in the world who can make an honest bowl of chili and I'm both of 'em." And thus the food cook-off mania was born. Now you, too, can be a world champion!

Not too hot, not too tame—an honest bowl of red you'll be proud to serve.

Chili meat* 2 pounds
Cooking oil 1/2 cup
Water (or beer) 1 1/2 cups
Tomato sauce 1 (8 oz.) can
Onions 2 small, chopped
Green pepper 1 medium, finely chopped
Garlic 5-6 cloves, minced
Oregano 1 teaspoon
Ground cumin 1 teaspoon
Chili powder 4 tablespoons
Salt 1 teaspoon
Sugar 1/2 teaspoon
Cayenne pepper
Jalapeno peppers 4-5 medium, chopped

In large skillet, braise meat in 1/4 cup oil until brown. Transfer meat to large kettle or electric slow cooker, leaving liquid in skillet. Add water and tomato sauce to meat, cook over low heat. Sauté onion, green pepper and garlic in remaining 1/4 cup oil and liquid in skillet. Add remaining dry ingredients and chopped jalapeno peppers with seeds removed. Simmer about 30 minutes then transfer to kettle. Simmer about 2 hours. Dip off grease that settles on top. (Cayenne and jalapeno peppers are the "zingers" in this recipe. Add both with caution.) Serves 8.

*Chili meat is coarsely ground round steak or well-trimmed chuck steak. It's usually labeled "chili meat" and is packaged in one to three-pound packs.

Terlingua Chili

Chuck roast 3 pounds
Ham butt 2-3 pounds
Ground beef 1 1/2 pounds
Italian sausage 1/2 pound
Beans 1 pound
Onion 1
Garlic 2 cloves
Bell pepper 1
Jalapeno peppers 2
Tomato sauce 15-ounce can
Tomatoes 16-ounce can, stewed
Salt and pepper to taste
Cheddar cheese

In Dutch oven or large pan, add roast, ham butt, ground beef and sausage with water to cover the meats. Bring to a boil. While meats are cooking, soak beans in large bowl till beans swell in size; set aside.

Chop onion, garlic, green pepper and add to boiling mixture with tomato sauce and stewed tomatoes. Simmer till meat falls away from bone.

Add beans and part of water they've soaked in. Simmer till beans are tender (24 hours in a crockpot set on medium setting). Transfer to a 2 1/2 quart baking dish, sprinkle with grated cheese and bake in a 325 degree oven about 20 minutes. Serves 6-10.

Terlingua may mean "three languages." Some people believe the languages are Spanish, English and Indian. Others feel it refers to the languages of the Apache, Comanche and Shawnee tribes, all three of whom have resided on Terlingua Creek. The town is world renowned as the location of the annual Wick Fowler Memorial Chili Cookoff (first Saturday and Sunday in November).

Bite-the-Bullet Locomotive Chili

Pinto beans 1/3 pound
Kidney beans 1/3 pound
Beans 1/3 pound, red or pink
Garlic 4 cloves
Mushrooms 1/3 pound
Celery 1 large stalk
Onions 2
Green pepper 1/2
Basil 1/4 cup, fresh
Parsley 1/4 cup, fresh
Olive oil
Chuck roast 1 pound, cubed
Tomatoes 3 (14 1/2 oz.) cans, stewed Italian
Bay leaf 1
Sugar 1 tablespoon
Chili powder 4 level tablespoons
Cumin 3 level tablespoons
Oregano 1 tablespoon
Cayenne 1 teaspoon
Marjoram 1 tablespoon
Tomato paste 2 (8 oz.) cans
Salt to taste

Combine beans and soak overnight in water to cover. Rinse beans next morning and set aside. Crush garlic. Slice mushrooms and celery. Chop onions, green pepper, basil and parsley separately.

In a large Dutch oven, heat oil and brown meat, onions, garlic, green pepper, mushrooms and celery until meat is cooked. Add rinsed beans to meat. Crush Italian tomatoes (use hands or electric beater) to keep seeds intact. Add tomatoes, bay leaf, sugar, spices and water (if needed) to barely cover. Simmer for at least an hour (until meat is tender). Turn off flame and stir in tomato paste. Taste and correct seasonings.

(Seeds of the Italian tomatoes should not be broken, for they may turn chili bitter. Adding tomato paste AFTER flame is turned off prevents chili from becoming bitter.) Serves 10-20.

Tex-Mex Chili

Reprinted from *Chili Lover's Cook Book**

Vegetable oil 3 tablespoons
Chuck roast 3 1/2 pounds, 1/2" cubes
Garlic 3 cloves, minced
Red peppers 1 teaspoon, crushed
Chili powder 6 tablespoons
Cumin seeds 1 1/2 teaspoon
Masa 3 tablespoons
Leaf oregano 1 tablespoon
Salt 2 teaspoons
Black pepper 1/2 teaspoon, coarse ground
Beef broth 13-ounce can
Tomato sauce 8-ounce can
Salsa 2-ounce can
Pinto beans 3 cups, cooked
Cheddar cheese sharp

Use lean boneless chuck. Add oil to cubed beef, and mix to coat all pieces. Heat a Dutch oven, add oiled beef cubes and stir over medium heat until beef loses pink color, but do NOT brown. Stir in garlic and crushed red peppers. Remove from heat.

Combine chili powder, cumin seed, masa (or all-purpose flour), oregano, salt and black pepper and sprinkle over beef cubes until well coated. Slowly add broth and tomato sauce to meat, stirring until well blended.

Return to heat, bring almost to boil, then reduce heat to low. Cover and simmer 1 1/2 hours; stir occasionally. Add chili salsa and beans (drained), and simmer 30 minutes more. Serve in heated bowls; garnish with grated cheese. Serves 6-8.

*Published by Golden West Publishers

Awful Good Texas Chili

Bacon 3 strips, thick
Beef 3 pounds lean, coarse ground
Onion 1 medium, chopped fine
Garlic 3 medium cloves, minced
Tomato paste 6-ounce can
Cumin 3 tablespoons, ground
Oregano 1 tablespoon, ground
Salt 1 tablespoon
Pepper 1 tablespoon, ground black
Beer* 12-ounce bottle
Chile pods 6-9 dried, red
Water 3 cups
(*Dark Mexican beer is best)

In a large, cast-iron kettle, fry bacon crisp. Remove and discard bacon saving the grease. Add meat, onion and garlic and sauté in bacon grease until meat is gray. Stir in tomato paste, then add spices and mix well through the meat. Pour in beer. Stir thoroughly and remove from heat.

Remove stems and seeds from dried chili pods. Boil in a covered saucepan with water for 15 minutes. Put peppers and water into blender and blend into thick sauce; pour sauce into kettle with meat; stir and simmer for 2 hours. Check after 1 1/2 hours. If chili needs thickening, add a tablespoon of masa harina. If chili is too thick, add water sparingly. For hotter chili, add cayenne pepper or Tabasco® sauce—sparingly. Serves 8.

Fiesta Chili

Reprinted from *Chili Lover's Cook Book*

Italian sausage 1 pound
Onions 2 medium
Chili peppers 2
Garlic 4 cloves
Tomatoes 2 (8 oz.) can
Bacon 8 slices
Ground chuck 1 pound
Tomato sauce 2 (8 oz.) cans
Kidney beans 2 (15 oz.) cans
Green onions 4
Cumin 2 teaspoons
Oregano 2 teaspoons
Basil 2 teaspoons
Salt to taste

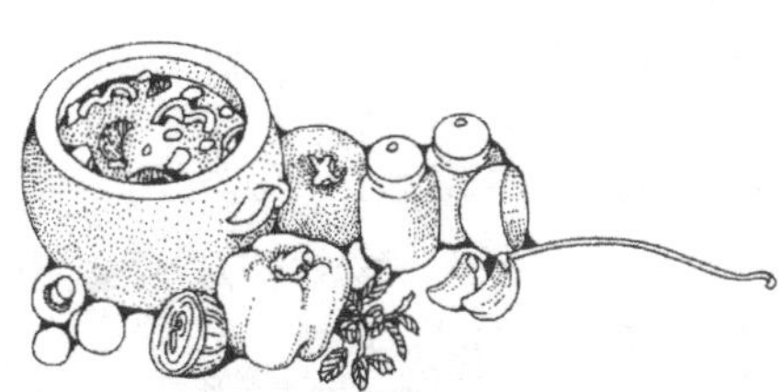

Slice the sausage. Chop onions and chili peppers very fine. Crush garlic cloves. Cut up canned tomatoes. Fry bacon until crisp; set strips aside. Drain all but one tablespoon bacon drippings and fry Italian sausage, ground chuck, onions and garlic until brown. Drain. Crumble bacon and add to ground chuck mixture along with remaining ingredients. Simmer for 30 minutes. Serves 6-8.

Chili cookoffs are a form of culinary competition popular on weekends throughout the year throughout Texas. A chili preparation duel which began in jest between humorist H. Allen Smith and journalist Wick Fowler in 1967 has mushroomed into a series of annual local and statewide competitions, culminating in the big international contest at Terlingua in early November. This event, known as the Wick Fowler Memorial Chili Cookoff, is sponsored by Chili Appreciation Society International.

Ranch Style Chili

Colleyville Woman's Club - Grapevine

Beef 1 pound lean
Green pepper 1 small chopped
Chili seasoning mix 1 package
Tomatoes 1 (16 oz.) can, cut up
Water 1/2 cup
Pinto beans 1/2 to 1 pound, optional

Brown beef in skillet, drain off excess fat. Blend in chili seasoning mix (below) and green pepper. Stir in tomatoes, water and beans. Bring to a boil. Reduce heat; cover and simmer 20-30 minutes.

Ranch Style Chili Seasoning Mix:

Flour 3 tablespoons
Paprika 1 1/2 teaspoon
Salt 1 teaspoon
Pepper 1/2 teaspoon crushed dried, optional
Onion 2 tablespoons instant minced
Chili powder 1 1/2 teaspoon
Cumin 1/2 teaspoon ground
Garlic 1/2 teaspoon minced
Sugar 1/2 teaspoon

Combine all ingredients and seal airtight. Repeat recipe to make as many packages as desired. Makes 1 package.

Among the legends of Texas, none is more colorful than the story of chili. Chili was first cooked in Texas border towns in the early 1800s. Every trail kit contained the necessary ingredients to prepare chili. It sustained the tired and cold cowboys when the weather was freezing. In 1893, "San Antonio Chilly" created a sensation at the Chicago World's Fair. It laid on the chiles and left out the beans. There are many ways to make chili. Each method has its advocates. The satisfying, delicious, rib-sticking quality is what chili recipes have in common.

Oatmeal Apple Muffins

Country Cottage Inn - Jean Sudderth - Dallas

Flour 1 cup
Sugar 4 tablespoons
Baking soda 1/2 teaspoon
Salt 1/2 teaspoon
Cinnamon 1 teaspoon
Oatmeal 3/4 cup
Corn oil 1/4 cup
Plain yogurt 1 cup
Apple 1/2 cup, chopped
Raisins 1/2 cup

Topping:
Orange juice 1 tablespoon
Orange rind 1/2 teaspoon, grated
Powdered sugar 1/2 cup

Combine first 6 ingredients. Add oil and yogurt. Mix in apple and raisins. Bake 400 degrees 15-20 minutes. Cool. Ice with orange topping.

Sweet Potato Biscuits

Castle Inn - Navasota

Preheat oven to 425 degrees.

Sweet potatoes 1 cup, mashed, cooked (1 medium potato in boiling water w/skin on about 15 minutes or fork tender—remove skin)
Sugar 1 cup
Milk 2/3 cup
Butter or margarine 4 tablespoons, melted
Flour 2 cups
Baking powder 4 teaspoons
Salt 1 teaspoon
Lots of butter or margarine

Mix sweet potatoes and sugar thoroughly, add milk and butter, add remaining dry ingredients, sifted together, to make a soft dough. Turn out on well floured board. Knead lightly until outside looks smooth. Roll out 1/2 inch thick, cut with floured biscuit cutter. Place on greased pans. Bake in 425 degree oven about 20 minutes, or until nicely browned. Serve with lots of butter or margarine.

No need to trek to Europe to find a castle when the Castle Inn offers accommodations in Navasota, Texas. The three-story Victorian mansion is available for lodging and breakfast. The Castle was built in 1893 with every modern convenience of the time. In 1983 it was further modernized and enlarged by its present owners.

Morado Cornbread

Anita K. Morado - Galveston

Cornbread mix 1 cup
Egg 1
Milk or buttermilk 1/2 cup
White onion grated
Green onions 2, chopped
Parsley
Okra 3 or 4 pods, sliced crossway
Green pepper 1/4, chopped

Mix all together and bake in a greased pan (sprinkle a little corn meal on bottom). Bake for about 20 minutes at 425 degrees. This mixture can be regulated by taking out some of the above vegetables and adding whatever you want. Taco seasoning may be added. Corn fritters can also be made from this recipe. Serves 3.

Nutt House Hot Water Cornbread

The Nutt House - Granbury

White cornmeal 1 cup
Yellow cornmeal 1 cup
Salt 1 teaspoon
Water 2 cups, boiling
Shortening 2 tablespoons
Baking powder 1/2 teaspoon
Water 2 tablespoons

Mix cormeals and salt thoroughly and pour in 2 cups boiling water containing 2 tablespoons shortening. This should produce a firm mound of dough. Set the dough aside and cool for 20 minutes. Work in 1/2 teaspoon of baking powder dissolved in 2 tablespoons water. Pinch off dough and pat into small round cakes. Fry immediately or refrigerate on wax paper for later cooking. Fry in deep fat hot enough to bubble freely over the cornbread. This cornbread should have a crisp crust on the outside yet be soft on the inside.

Mini Cinnamons

Wild Briar - The Country Inn at Edom - Ben Wheeler

Bread 16 slices, decrusted
Vanilla 1 teaspoon
Egg 1
Sugar 1/2 cup
Cream cheese 8 ounce

Frosting:
Sugar 1 cup
Cinnamon 2 tablespoons

Spread mixture of vanilla, egg, cream cheese and 1/2 cup sugar on each bread slice. Roll up as a jelly roll. Dip each roll into melted margarine and then into mixture of cinnamon and the 1 cup of sugar. Place rolls on cookie sheet, cover with foil and freeze 2-3 hours. When firm, slice rolls into bite-size pieces, about 5 to a roll. You may either roll in foil paper and refreeze to use later or heat at 350 degrees for 10-15 minutes. We turn ours over after about 10 minutes when they are brown on both sides. Watch carefully until you are sure how your oven cooks.

Pumpkin Rice Bread

Flour 3 1/2 cups
Baking soda 2 teaspoons
Salt 1 teaspoon
Cinnamon 1 teaspoon
Nutmeg 1 teaspoon
Sugar 3 cups
Oil 1 cup
Eggs 4, beaten
Water 2/3 cup
Pumpkin 2 cups
Pecans 1/2 cup, chopped
Raisins 1/2 cup, chopped
Rice 1 1/2 cups, cooked

Sift all dry ingredients in large bowl. Add oil, eggs, water and pumpkin, mixing well. Fold in pecans, raisins and rice. Pour into lightly greased tube pan and bake at 325 degrees for 1 hour.

Zucchini Bread

Zella Landfair - San Marcos

Eggs 3
Zucchini 2 cups, grated
Oil 1 cup
Sugar 2 cups
Vanilla 2 teaspoons
Flour 3 cups
Salt 1 teaspoon
Baking powder 1 teaspoon
Cinnamon 1 teaspoon
Nuts 1/2 cup or more, chopped

Beat eggs, add zucchini, oil, sugar and vanilla. Beat well or cream. Sift dry ingredients and add to creamed mixture. Mix until moistened and add nuts. Bake in greased 9 x 5 inch loaf pans at 325 degrees until done, about 1 hour. Makes 2 loaves.

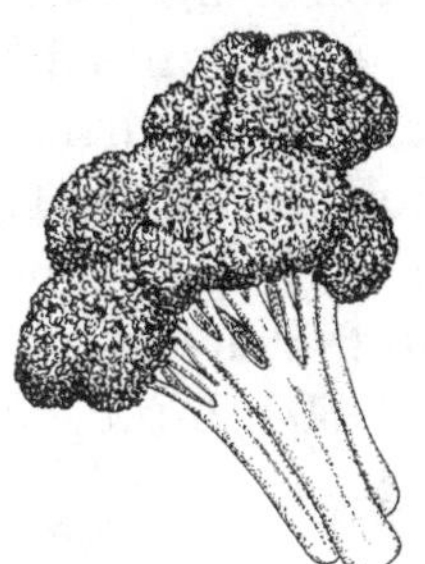

Broccoli Cornbread

Barbara Smith - Fort Worth

Cornbread mix 2 (8 1/2 oz.) boxes
Cottage cheese 1 (16 oz.) carton
Butter or margarine 1 stick, melted
Eggs 5, beaten
Frozen chopped broccoli 1 (8 oz.) package, thawed

Preheat oven to 350 degrees. Mix all ingredients well. Pour mixture into well-greased 9 x 13 inch pan or large iron skillet. Bake for 20-25 minutes.

Best Ever Rolls

Odie L. Crumby - Bonham

Dry yeast 2 packages
Water 3 tablespoons, warm (105-115 degrees)
Sugar 1/2 cup
Shortening 1/2 cup, melted
Eggs 2, beaten
Water 1 cup warm (105-115 degrees)
Salt 1 teaspoon
Flour 4 1/2 - 5 cups, divided
Butter or margarine 1/4 cup plus 2 tablespoons, softened

Dissolve yeast in 3 tablespoons warm water in large mixing bowl; let stand 5 minutes. Add sugar, shortening, eggs, 1 cup warm water, salt and 2 cups flour. Beat with electric mixer 1 minute. Gradually stir in remaining flour to make a soft dough. Turn dough onto a floured board, knead 4 minutes or until smooth and elastic. Shape dough into a ball, place in a well-greased bowl to rise. Cover and let rise 1 hour. Punch down, divide into 3 equal parts. Roll each into a 12-inch circle. Spread with melted butter. Cut each circle into 6-8 wedges. Roll each wedge beginning at wide end. Place on greased baking sheets, point side down. Let rise 45-60 minutes. Bake at 400 degrees for 10-12 minutes. Serves 8.

Wheatberry Bread

Sandy Ayres - Fort Worth

Combine in order:

Butter 1/2 cup
Salt 3 teaspoons
Baking soda 1/4 teaspoon
Honey 1/2 cup
Wheat germ 1/2 cup
Bran 1/2 cup
Raisins 1 cup, ground or finely minced
Water 2 cups, boiling

Set aside to cool. Then add and mix:

Eggs 2 beaten
Dry yeast 2 packages, dissolved in 1/2 cup warm water

Add and work into mixture:

Whole wheat flour 3 1/2 - 4 cups
Unbleached white flour 4 - 4 1/2 cups

Turn dough onto lightly floured surface and knead 10 minutes, working in extra flour if dough is too sticky. Let rise in warm place until doubled in bulk (approximately 2 hours). Punch down and knead five minutes. Divide dough in half and place in two greased one-pound loaf tins. Let rise until almost doubled in bulk (approximately 1 1/2 hours). Bake at 400 degrees 35-45 minutes.

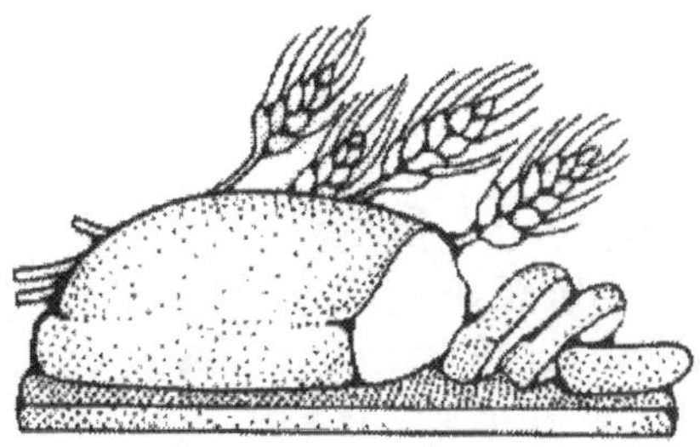

Salad Bread

Beverly McClatchy - Midland

Biscuits 3 cans
Cheddar cheese 1/2 cup, grated
Margarine 1 1/2 - 2 sticks
Pimentos 1/2 small jar

Mix 2-3 of the following:

Green pepper 3/4 cup, chopped
Onion 3/4 cup, chopped
Celery 3/4 cup, chopped
Chives 3/4 cup, chopped
Parsley 3/4 cup, chopped

Melt margarine and sauté chosen chopped vegetables. Cut biscuits into quarters. Mix all together thoroughly. Bake in bundt pan or tube pan at 400 degrees 10-15 minutes. Serves 6-8.

Tip: Tear bread apart rather than cutting. Serve hot.

Texmati Brown Rice Bread

Texmati Brand Rice Products - Alvin

Milk 1 1/4 cups, scalded
Shortening 1/4 cup
Brown sugar 3 tablespoons
Salt 1 teaspoon
Texmati® Brown Rice 3 cups, cooked
Active dry yeast 2 packages
All-purpose flour 2 cups
Whole wheat flour 2 cups

Pour 1 cup scalded milk over shortening, sugar and salt. Add cooked rice. Dissolve yeast in cooled 1/4 cup scalded milk, stir into rice mixture. Work in flour to make a firm dough. Turn out on floured board and knead until smooth and elastic. Place in greased bowl, cover and let rise until doubled. Punch down and knead 2-3 minutes. Shape into loaves and place in well greased loaf pans. Cover, let rise again until doubled in bulk, then brush tops with melted butter and bake at 375 degrees for 40-45 minutes. Makes 2 loaves.

Wurstfest Sausage Rolls

Imperial Sugar Company - Sugar Land

These soft warm rolls will have you dancing right in your own kitchen to polka music from the Wurstfest.

Dry yeast 1 package or 1 cake yeast
Warm water 1 tablespoon
Sugar 1 teaspoon
Shortening 1/2 cup
Sugar 1/2 cup
Salt 1 teaspoon
Hot water 1 cup
Eggs 3, beaten
Flour 4 - 4 1/2 cups
Wurst sausage cut in strips 1 1/2" x 1/2"

Combine yeast, warm water and sugar; set aside. Combine shortening, sugar, salt, hot tap water and eggs and beat well. Add yeast mixture. Add 2 cups of the flour and beat well. Stir in another 2 - 2 1/2 cups of the flour to make a soft dough. Refrigerate covered dough in large mixing bowl overnight. Divide dough into three portions. Roll one portion of dough into circle 1/4" thick and cut with biscuit cutter into 2" diameter circles. Simmer sausages in covered pan about 5 minutes. Place sausages in centers of circles of dough. Moisten edges of dough with water, lap one side of dough over sausage and press edges of dough together to seal. Repeat with remaining dough. Place rolls on greased cookie sheet and let rise about 1 1/2 hours, or until doubled. Bake in preheated 350 degree oven about 10-12 minutes, or until golden brown. Makes about 36 rolls.

The heritage and customs of our early pioneers have had a profound effect on Texas culture and it is not unusual to find fests and festivals dedicated to preserving these old world traditions. Here is a sampling of the authentic foods you are likely to find at an Oktoberfest in Houston, the Wurstfest in New Braunfels or at a Night in Old Fredericksburg, usually held on the third weekend in July. Happy eating!

Border Butterflake Biscuits

Imperial Sugar Company - Sugar Land

All-purpose flour 2 cups
Baking powder 1 tablespoon
Salt 3/4 teaspoon
Sugar 1 tablespoon
Butter or margarine 1/2 cup (1 stick) plus 2 tablespoons
Eggs 2, well beaten
Milk 1/3 cup, cold

Sift dry ingredients together; cut butter or margarine into mixture with pastry blender. Mix well beaten eggs and milk, add to mixture and mix lightly with fork. Shape dough into ball and turn out on lightly floured surface. With rolling pin, lightly roll dough into rectangle about 1/2 inch thick. Fold dough in thirds and roll into oblong two more times. With dough 1/2 inch thick, cut into two-inch diameter biscuits. Bake on ungreased baking sheet in preheated 475 degree oven until biscuits are puffed and golden brown. Makes 24 two-inch biscuits.

Note: The secret of success in making this recipe is to handle the dough very gently, both in mixing and rolling out the dough.

Bran Muffins

Norton Brackenridge House - San Antonio

Raisin bran cereal 10 ounces
Flour 5 cups
Sugar 3 cups
Baking powder 3 teaspoons
Salt 2 teaspoons
Buttermilk 1 quart
Cooking oil 1 cup
Eggs 4, beaten

Mix dry ingredients in large bowl. Add liquids. Bake in muffin tins 15-20 minutes at 400 degrees. Batter will keep in refrigerator up to 6 weeks.

It can be said that Tex-Mex cuisine is Mexican-style cooking with a Texas influence. As styles of Mexican cooking vary throughout the Mexican states, so do they vary in the four border states, and even within each state. Tex-Mex is not a single cuisine, but several styles that have become famous throughout the world as "Tex-Mex." They may use flour or corn tortillas, a variety of chile peppers, various fillings in tacos, enchiladas, burritos, tostadas and tamales. Tex-Mex cooks use tomatillas and cilantro to spice up their sauces or table salsas. Chiles may be mild or hot; chile powder may be used liberally or sparingly to add the desired "fire" to the pot. Other ingredients include corn, avocado, onion, garlic, rice, beans, chocolate, cheese, chicken, beef, pork, eggs and vegetables.

Tortilla Cups

Mansion on Turtle Creek - Dallas

Corn tortillas
Oil for deep frying

With a 2-inch round biscuit cutter punch out mini-tortillas. Heat frying oil to 325 degrees. Float a circle of tortilla on the oil, then with a small ladle in the center of each push them below the surface and hold them there until crisp, about 30 seconds. Remove and invert onto paper toweling to drain.

Rice Bake

Cornmeal 1 cup
Salt 1/2 teaspoon
Baking soda 1/2 teaspoon
Rice, white or brown 2 cups, cooked
Low-fat milk 1 cup
Creamed style corn 1 (8 3/4 oz.) can
Onion 1/2 cup, chopped
Green chiles 1 (4 oz.) can, chopped
Vegetable oil 1 tablespoon
Monterey Jack cheese shredded 3/4 cup

Combine cornmeal, salt and soda in bowl, stirring well. Add remaining ingredients except cheese. Pour into 12 x 8 x 2 inch baking pan that has been coated with cooking spray. Bake at 350 degrees for 45 minutes or until lightly browned. Sprinkle cheese on top, and return to oven till cheese melts. Serves 8-10.

Stubby's West Texas Posole

Mike "Stubby" Arnold - Midland

White hominy 1 (16 oz.) can
Golden hominy 1 (16 oz.) can
Green chiles 2 (4 oz.) cans, chopped
Cream cheese 3 ounces
Velveeta® cheese 4 ounces
Pimentos 2 tablespoons
Garlic powder 1 teaspoon
Red pepper (cayenne) to taste

Drain both cans of hominy. Place in large sauce pan over low heat. Add remaining ingredients: chopped green chiles, pimentos, cream cheese, Velveeta cheese and garlic powder. Heat slowly, stirring often, until both cheeses are well blended and all ingredients are well mixed. Add red pepper to taste. (Be careful now. This stuff is really hot!!) And enjoy. Serves 6-8.

Tip: Prepare 1 hour before serving. Let stand in covered dish or sauce pan. Reheat 5 minutes before serving.

Spanish Rice

Carmen Rodriguez - San Marcos

Long grain rice 3/4 cup
Oil 2 tablespoons
Onion 1/4 cup, chopped
Garlic clove 1
Bell pepper 1 small, chopped
Cumin powder 1/2 teaspoon
Salt 1 1/2 teaspoon
Black pepper 1/2 teaspoon
Tomato sauce 1/2 small can
Water 2 1/2 or 3 cups

In 10 inch skillet fry rice in oil on low heat until pink. Have ready chopped onion, bell pepper and garlic. Stir in the rest of ingredients. Cover and simmer about 40-45 minutes on low-medium heat. Makes 4 1/3 cup servings.

Cowboy Lasagna

Shirley Baumbach - Edinburg

Ground beef 2 pounds
Chili powder 1 tablespoon
Onion 1 large, chopped
Cream of chicken soup 2 cans
Enchilada sauce 1 can
Tortilla chips 1 (10 oz.) bag
Cheddar cheese 1 (10 oz.) bag, grated

Brown ground beef, add chili powder and chopped onion. Add soup and enchilada sauce, mixing well. In a 2 quart casserole dish, layer beef mixture, chips, cheese, beef mixture, chips and cheese, ending with cheese on top. Bake at 350 degrees oven for 40 minutes or microwave at high power for 15 minutes. Serves 5.

Beef Enchiladas

Carmen Rodriguez - San Marcos

Vegetable Shortening 4 tablespoons
Corn tortillas 12
Lean ground hamburger meat 1 1/2 pound
Onion 1 medium, chopped fine
Garlic clove 1, chopped fine
Flour 1/4 cup and 1 tablespoon
Chili powder 2 1/2 tablespoons
Cumin powder 1 teaspoon
Water 2 cups
Salt 1 1/2 teaspoon
Black pepper 1/4 teaspoon
Mild cheddar cheese 1 1/2 pounds, grated

In 8 inch skillet, heat 3 tablespoons vegetable shortening and fry tortillas 1 at a time. Fry for just a few seconds, turn once and remove softened tortilla. Fry 1 at a time and be ready to roll.

Brown meat in 10 inch skillet and 1 tablespoon of vegetable shortening. Stir in 1/3 cup onions and cook for 5 minutes. Cover and cook at medium heat. Add garlic and flour, chili powder, stir and cook and add cumin powder. Stir and add 2 cups of water. Add salt and pepper and stir. Cover and cook for 15 minutes.

Have cheese, the rest of onion, meat and fried tortillas ready to roll. In each tortilla put 3 tablespoons meat mixture. Sprinkle cheese and onion, roll and put in an oblong oven-proof baking dish. Spread meat lightly and sprinkle cheese. Put in microwave, cover with plastic wrap. Poke 1 or 2 holes and set at 2 minutes on high temperature. Serve hot with lettuce and tomato salad and beans and Spanish rice. Makes 12 enchiladas.

One mile northwest of San Marcos are the headwaters of the San Marcos River. Created by the Balcones Fault, a fault line deep within the earth, is San Marcos Spring, from which the river flows. The falls produce 200 million gallons of ice-cold water daily.

Stuffed Chicken Breast with Enchilada Sauce

Carol Barclay - Portland

Whole chicken breasts 4, boned and skinned
Green chiles 4 to 5, seeded and chopped
Bulk chorizo sausage 1/4 pound, cooked and drained well
Monterey Jack cheese 1/2 pound, cut into 4 slices
Dry bread crumbs 1/2 cup, fine
Chili powder 1 tablespoon
Ground cumin 1/2 teaspoon
Salt and pepper to taste
Butter 6 tablespoons, melted
Green onion tops chopped
Cilantro minced fresh

Enchilada Sauce:
Tomato sauce 1 (8 oz.) can
Ground cumin 1 teaspoon
Chili powder 1 teaspoon
Coriander 1/2 teaspoon, ground
Black pepper 1/4 teaspoon, freshly ground
Salt and pepper to taste

Combine all sauce ingredients and heat to boiling. Pound chicken breasts between sheets of wax paper until thin. Spread each piece with equal amounts of chiles and chorizo. Top with cheese slice and roll up. Combine bread crumbs, chili powder, cumin, salt and pepper. Dip each chicken breast in melted butter and roll in crumb mixture. Place breasts seam side down in baking dish. Chill for at least 1 hour. Bake chicken at 400 degrees for 30 minutes. Pour enchilada sauce over baked chicken. Garnish with green onion and cilantro. Serves 4.

Daniel's Enchilada Casserole

George Douglass - Colleyville

Onion 1 medium diced
Lean ground chuck 1 1/2 pounds
Enchilada Sauce 1 can
Cream of chicken soup 1 can
Green chiles 1 (4 oz.) can chopped
Corn tortillas 12
Cheddar cheese 8 ounces shredded

Dice onion and sauté with meat. Brown, then drain all excess fat. Add all canned items. Cook on low heat until mixture is real smooth. Dip corn tortillas in hot oil so they are flexible. In a 9 x 13 x 2 pan cover the bottom with corn tortillas, then a layer of meat sauce. Make 2 more layers of tortillas and meat sauce. Preheat oven to 325 degrees. Cook for approximately 10 minutes or until heated through. Remove from oven, cover with shredded cheese. Return to oven until cheese melts. Serves 6.

Tip: After cool, cut into squares. Freezes well.

Taco Soup

Vernie Bailey - Kemp

Corn 1 can
Ranch style beans 1 can
Pinto beans 1 can
Tomatoes 1 (32 oz.) can, Mexican style
Green chiles 1 (16 oz.) can
Rotel® hot spiced tomatoes chopped
Taco mix 1 package
Hidden Valley® ranch salad dressing mix 1 package dry

Mix all of the ingredients together well. Cook 30 minutes. Serves 6-8.

Party Layered Pie

Adele Tibbs - Big Spring

Ground meat 1 1/2 pounds
Chili powder 1 tablespoon
Cumin 1 teaspoon
Salt & pepper 1 teaspoon
Garlic powder 1/2 teaspoon
Red pepper 1/2 teaspoon
Tomatoes 16 ounce can, chopped
Tortillas 12

Brown meat, drain, add rest of seasonings and tomatoes, then heat. Line 13 x 9 baking dish with tortillas. Pour meat mixture over tortillas. Cover with rest of tortillas and set aside. Mix and pour the following over the tortillas:

Cottage cheese 2 cups small
Monterey Jack cheese 8 ounces with peppers
Egg 1

Bake at 350 degrees for 30 minutes. When done decorate in diagonal strips with the following, alternating:

Tomatoes 1/2 cup fresh
Cheddar cheese 1/2 cup
Green onions 1/2 cup
Lettuce 2 cups, shredded
Ripe olives 1/4 cup, sliced

Big Spring was a convenient camping site for early exploration of western Texas. It was also a place where Comanche and Shawnee would meet and barter or socialize. Animals of the wilderness—coyotes, buffalo, wolves and wild mustangs—enjoyed it as a watering hole. Early known by several other names, it became Big Spring in 1882.

Layered Fiesta Dip

Amigos Canning Company - San Antonio

Amigos® Bean Dip 2 (9 oz.) cans
Avocados 6, mashed
Lemon juice 2 tablespoons
Amigos® Picante Sauce 1 can
Sour cream 1 pint
Black olives 1 (4 1/2 oz.) can, chopped
Green onions 1 bunch, chopped
Tomato 1 large, chopped
Cheddar cheese 2 cups, shredded

In a 9 x 13 inch glass pan spread bean dip. Mix avocados, lemon juice and picante sauce; spread over bean dip. Spread sour cream over avocado mixture and top with olive, onions, tomatoes and cheese. Serve with your favorite chips.

Variation: Add 1/4 cup chopped green olives to top of dish, or use 2 cartons of avocado dip in place of avocados or use 1 can of nacho cheese dip in place of shredded cheddar cheese.

Mexican Cheese Dip

Amigos Canning Company - San Antonio

Amigos® Nacho Cheese Dip 2 cans
Ground beef 1/2 pound
Sausage 1/2 pound
Amigos® Picante Sauce 1 can
Onion soup mix 1 envelope
Cream of mushroom soup 1 can

In a large saucepan melt cheese. Brown ground beef and sausage together and drain. Add meat to nacho cheese dip. Mix in picante sauce, onion soup mix and mushroom soup. Heat until warm. Pour into crockpot to keep warm. Serve with corn chips. Also great over rice.

Zesty Bean Dip

Amigos Canning Company - San Antonio

Amigos® Bean Dip 2 (9 oz.) cans
Sour cream 1 cup
Jalapenos 3 to 5, seeded and chopped

Mix all ingredients together in a saucepan. Heat on top of stove until very hot. Serve.

Note: Keep sour cream from curdling by allowing it to come to room temperature before adding it to hot mixtures.

Chili Relleno

Barbara Smith - Fort Worth

Cheddar cheese 1 pound grated
Jack cheese 1 pound grated
Whole green chiles 3 (4 oz.) cans (I use 4 cans)
Eggs 3
Evaporated milk 1 (13 oz.) can
Flour 3 tablespoons
Tomato sauce 1 (8 oz.) can

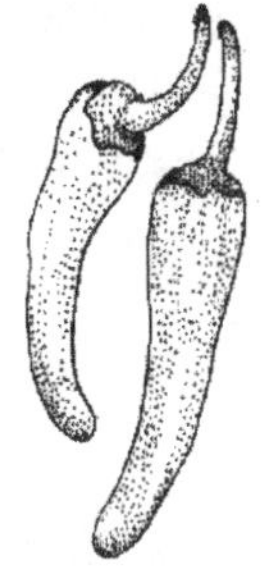

In 9 x 13 x 2 oven-proof baking dish, layer:

1/2 chiles
1/2 Jack cheese
1/2 cheddar cheese
1/2 chiles
1/2 cheddar cheese

Mix batter made up of eggs, milk and flour and pour over layered stuff. Bake at 375 degrees for 25 minutes. Add rest of Jack cheese, pour tomato sauce over top and bake 20-25 minutes longer.

Sanford Style Picante Sauce

Mark M. Sanford - Comfort

Tomato sauce 1 (8 oz.) can
Tomatoes 2 large fresh diced
Green chiles 1 small can diced
Tomato sauce 1 can (Mexican style)
Dried red peppers 1/2 teaspoon or more, crushed
Coarse ground black pepper 1/2 teaspoon
Green onions 1 bunch chopped
Serrano peppers 2-5 (flavor to taste)
Garlic 2 medium cloves, chopped

Add regular tomato sauce, tomatoes, green chiles, Mexican tomato sauce, red peppers and black pepper in a large bowl. In a blender add green onions, serrano peppers and garlic and blend until consistency is well mashed (usually 15 seconds). Add blender ingredients into mixture. Mix all ingredients together. Ready to use. Keep any unused sauce in refrigerator (up to 3 weeks).

Tip: Experimentation with the above basic ingredients is the key to success. Everyone's taste varies—the hotter your preference, just add or subtract red peppers and serrano peppers. Stores well in jars. May be "canned" by hot bath method, following same procedure as for canned tomatoes. May be used as a sauce or served with your favorite chips.

Texas state law makes it unlawful for anyone to disturb in any way historic or prehistoric, archaeological or paleontological sites, or any historic marker situated on lands controlled by the State of Texas. Take all the photographs you like, but help preserve Texas heritage for future generations.

Turkey Rice Casserole

Texmati Brands Rice Products - Alvin

Texmati® Rice 2 cups white or brown cooked
Turkey 2 cups cooked cubed
Zucchini 2 medium, cut into 1/4 inch rounds
Jack cheese 3/4 cup shredded
Green chiles 1 (4 oz.) can chopped, drained
Tomatoes 2 medium, halved lengthwise then sliced crosswise

Topping:
Sour cream 1 cup
Onion 1/3 cup chopped
Salt 1/2 teaspoon
Oregano 1/4 teaspoon
Pepper to taste
Jack or cheddar cheese 3/4 cup shredded

Spread rice in greased 2 quart baking dish. Top with remaining ingredients, layering. Mix all topping ingredients together except for the cheese and spread over casserole. Sprinkle with cheese. Bake at 350 degrees for 30 minutes. Serves 6.

Chicken Rice Squares

Texmati Brands Rice Products - Alvin

Butter 2 tablespoons
Onion 1 small
Garlic clove 1 minced
Chicken broth 2 cups
Salt 1 teaspoon
Texmati® Rice 1 cup uncooked
Eggs 3
Cream 3/4 cup heavy
Cayenne pepper 1/4 teaspoon
Chicken 1 cooked, deboned and chopped
Spinach 2 (10 oz.) packages, thawed and pressed dry
Cheddar cheese 3/4 cup grated

Melt butter in saucepan, add onion and garlic and sauté. Add chicken broth and salt; bring to a boil and stir in rice. Return to a boil then cover and simmer 15-20 minutes. In large bowl beat together eggs, cream and cayenne. Add chicken, rice mixture, spinach and 1/2 cup cheese. Mix well and pour into greased baking pan. Pack firmly. Sprinkle with 1/4 cup cheese. Cover with foil and bake at 350 degrees for 30 minutes. Remove foil and continue baking 10 minutes longer. Serves 8.

Texas Hash

Carmen Dougherty - Marion

Ground meat 1 pound
Onions 1 1/2 large, thinly sliced
Green pepper 1 large, chopped
Tomatoes 1 (16 oz.) can
Rice 1/2 cup, uncooked
Salt 2 teaspoons
Chili powder 1-2 teaspoons
Black pepper 1/8 teaspoon

In a large skillet, cook and stir meat, onion and green pepper until meat is brown and vegetables are tender. Drain fat. Stir in tomatoes, rice, salt, chili powder and pepper. Heat thoroughly. Pour into an ungreased 2 quart casserole. Cover. Bake 1 hour at 350 degrees. Serves 4.

Sweet and Sour Pork with Pineapple and Peppers

Myra Goodman - Texas City

Green peppers 2, cut into sections
Cucumber 1 medium
Pineapple cut into sections
Tomato 1 large, cut into sections
Pork 1 1/2 pounds
Eggs 2
Flour 5 tablespoons
Oil 16 ounces, peanut or salad oil
Salt 1/2 teaspoon

Cut the green peppers, cucumber, pineapple and tomato into sections. Chop the pork into same size, though not the same shape (remove fat).

Dip pork in whipped eggs before rolling in flour. Heat the oil until boiling. Fry each piece of pork until brown and crispy. Drain well. All frying must be done when oil is boiling. Leave only 4 tablespoons of oil in the pan and pour in the green pepper, tomato, pineapple and cucumber. Add salt and stir for 1 minute. Mix with fried pork. Heat the Sweet and Sour Sauce (below) and pour on top of pork, mixing well. Serve piping hot. Serves 4-6.

Sweet and Sour Sauce:

Sugar 3/4 cup
Soy sauce 1/4 cup
Vinegar 1/3 cup
Water 2/3 cup
Tomato sauce 1 tablespoon, for coloring
Cornstarch 1 1/2 tablespoons

Cook over low heat until thickened, stirring constantly.

Mama's Chicken

Tami Thomas - Texas City

Margarine 2 tablespoons
Chicken 4 half breasts, skinned and boned
Yellow onion 1 medium, sliced and separated into rings
Mushrooms 1 1/2 cups, sliced
White wine 1/2 cup
Provolone cheese 2 sliced, cut in half

Melt margarine in deep skillet and add chicken. Cook until lightly browned on both sides. Arrange onions and mushrooms over chicken and pour wine over all. Cover and simmer until vegetables are tender, about 15 minutes. Remove from heat. Place provolone cheese on top of chicken, cover and let steam until melted. Serves 4.

Stir Fry Pepper Steak

Enell Helen Creel - Texas City

Salt and pepper
Round steak 1 medium-sized, cut into thin slices
Soy sauce 6 tablespoons
Worcestershire sauce 2 tablespoons
Olive oil 7 tablespoons
Bell peppers 2 medium, cut into large pieces
Onion 1 large, cut into large pieces
Carrots 1 or 2 medium, cut into small pieces
Ground ginger 1/4 teaspoon
Green peas 1/2 box, frozen
3-minute rice 1 small box
Chinese noodles 1 large can or package

Salt and pepper steak and marinate in soy sauce and Worcestershire sauce for 15 minutes. In electric wok, put olive oil and heat. Stir fry for about 30 minutes. Add bell pepper, onion and carrots. Then add ground ginger and green peas. Cook until vegetables are tender yet crunchy. Cook rice as directed. When all is done, put rice and then the meat mixture in oblong dish. Top with Chinese noodles. Serves 8.

Chicken Broccoli Casserole

Enell Helen Creel - Texas City

Chicken breasts 3-4
Broccoli 1 bunch, cut up
Mayonnaise 1 cup
Cream of mushroom soup 2 cans
Lemon juice 1 1/2 teaspoon
Seasoned bread crumbs 3/4 package
Butter 1/4 to 1/2 pound

Bake chicken at 300 degrees for 1 hour. Cut up into bite-size pieces. Cook broccoli for 15 minutes. Layer chicken and broccoli in casserole. Pour mixture of mayonnaise, mushroom soup and lemon juice over chicken and broccoli. Toss bread crumbs in melted butter. Mix some with casserole and put the rest on top. Bake at 350 degrees for 30-40 minutes. Serves 6.

Sizzling Shrimp

Edith Eason - Texas City

Olive oil 1 1/2 cups
Salt 1 tablespoon
Ketchup 1/2 cup
Paprika 1 teaspoon
Garlic cloves 3, sliced
Onion 1/2 small, minced
Parsley 1 tablespoon
Lemon juice 1 tablespoon
Shrimp 3 pounds, large fresh

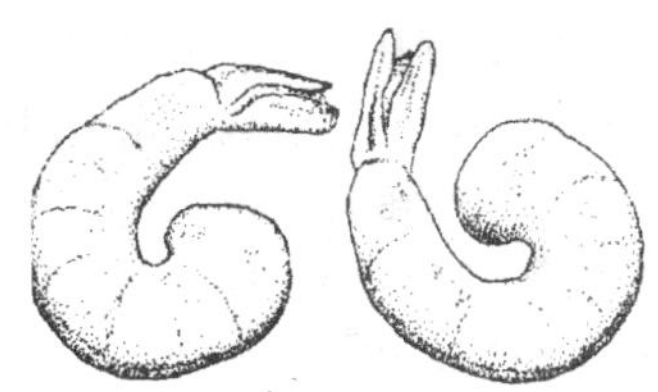

Combine oil, salt, ketchup, paprika, garlic, onion, lemon juice and parsley. Peel and clean shrimp, leaving tails on. Place shrimp in sauce in refrigerator to marinate at least 1 hour. Arrange shrimp on skewers, place on broiler and brush with sauce. Broil 4 inches from heat for 10 minutes or grill over charcoal. Turn and baste shrimp at least once during broiling period. Serves 6.

Pineapple Chicken Cordon Bleu

Larry Eason - Texas City

Pineapple slices 8-ounce can, juice packed, drained
Chicken breasts 2 halves, skinned and boned
Flour 2 tablespoons
Onion salt 1/2 teaspoon
Butter 1 tablespoon
Boiled ham 2 thin slices (2 oz.)
Cheddar cheese sauce 1 cup, package mix or use recipe below

Pound chicken to 1/2 inch thickness. Dredge chicken in combined flour and onion salt. Cook in butter on each side until browned, about 10 minutes. Top each with ham slice and heat through. Remove to serving platter or plate.

Cook pineapple until heated through. Top each chicken breast with 2 slices pineapple. Pour 1/2 cup cheese over each. Serves 2.

Cheddar Cheese Sauce:

Flour 1 tablespoon
Butter 1 tablespoon
Milk 1 cup
Cheddar cheese 1/4 cup, finely grated, sharp
Salt and pepper to taste

In small saucepan melt butter, add flour and stir. Let this bubble up, then remove from heat. Add milk all at once. Stir or whisk over low heat until smooth and beginning to thicken. Add cheese and stir.

Cajun Chicken with Spicy Salsa

Jerry Jares - Santa Fe

Hot sauce 1/3 cup
Lemon juice 2 tablespoons
Honey 1 tablespoon
Sage 2 teaspoons
Chicken parts 2 1/2 to 3 1/2 pounds, skinned
Salt 1/2 teaspoon
Ground red pepper 1 teaspoon
Chili powder 1 teaspoon
Paprika 1 teaspoon
Cooking spray
Onion 1 medium to large, chopped
Green bell pepper 1/2, chopped
Celery 1/2 cup, finely chopped
Orange juice 6-ounce can, unsweetened
Tomato paste 2 tablespoons
Honey 2 tablespoons
Worcestershire sauce 1 tablespoon
Orange peel 1 long curl
Ground ginger 1/4 teaspoon

Mix the first four ingredients together. Pour over skinned chicken pieces and marinate at least 3 hours or overnight (in the refrigerator). Preheat oven to 350 degrees. Remove chicken from marinade and arrange pieces in a 9 x 13 pan. Combine salt, red pepper, chili powder and paprika and sprinkle over chicken. Generously apply cooking spray to skillet. Over medium-high heat, sauté onions, bell pepper and celery for 5 minutes. Stir occasionally.

Add all remaining ingredients to skillet and cook, stirring for 5 minutes longer or until sauce thickens. Remove from heat and pour over chicken.

Cover with aluminum foil and bake for 30 minutes. Turn chicken over and baste with sauce. Bake uncovered for 3 minutes longer or until chicken is done. Remove orange peel curl and adjust seasonings. Serve chicken with salsa over it. This is a low-fat, low-calorie recipe. Serves 4.

Pan Seared Veal Chop with Apple-Bourbon Sauce

The Mansion on Turtle Creek - Dallas

Veal chops four 8-ounce center cut, with rib bone attached (this bone must be completely clean of all meat)
Salt to taste
Peanut oil 3 tablespoons
Apple-Bourbon Sauce (recipe follows)

Preheat oven to 375 degrees. Season each chop with salt. Heat oil in a large oven-proof sauté pan over medium high heat until small wisps of smoke appear. Carefully place each chop into the pan, with side to be presented down. Cook on first side about 4 minutes, or until surface is crusty and browned. Turn chops, place pan in oven. Cook for 12 minutes or until desired doneness. Remove pan from oven and place chops on warm platter until served.

Apple-Bourbon Sauce:

Veal bones 1 pound, cut into sections from the shank
Peanut oil 2 tablespoons
Onion 1 medium sized, peeled and sliced
Mushrooms 4 large white, cleaned and sliced
Shallots 4, peeled and roughly chopped
Kentucky Bourbon 1/4 cup
Granny Smith apples 3, cored and sliced
Chicken stock 4 cups
Thyme 4 sprigs fresh
Sage 3 sprigs fresh
Black peppercorns 2 teaspoons cracked
Kentucky Bourbon 1/8 cup
Salt, lemon juice to taste

Preheat oven to 375 degrees. Place bones in a roasting pan and sprinkle with a teaspoon of peanut oil. Roast until bones are a deep golden brown about 12 minutes (stir once during roasting). When done, set aside. Heat remaining oil in a large saucepan. When hot, add onion and sauté until browned about ten minutes. Then add mushrooms, shallots, two of the apples,

(continued on next page)

and sauté three minutes. Add the 1/4 cup bourbon and stir well, scraping the bottom of the pan. Incorporate any browned bits of vegetables. Next add the browned bones, thyme, sage, chicken stock and pepper. Bring to a boil, skim carefully and simmer gently for 30 minutes. Remove bones from sauce, add the reserved apples and cook an additional 10 minutes. Pour sauce (including apples and vegetables) into a blender jar and carefully blend for 10-15 seconds. Strain sauce into a sauce container through a coarse strainer pressing well to pass as much pulp as possible through. Add 1/8 cup bourbon to refresh and season with salt and lemon juice to taste. Keep warm until served. Serves 4.

South of the Border Spaghetti

Carol Barclay - Portland

Onions 2 medium, chopped
Garlic clove 1, minced
Bell pepper 1 medium, chopped
Bacon drippings 3 tablespoons
Ground beef 1 pound
Chili powder 2 tablespoons
Salt 1 teaspoon
Paprika
Ketchup 1 tablespoon
Rotel® tomatoes and green chiles 1 (10 oz.) can
Worcestershire sauce 2 tablespoons
Thin spaghetti 1 (8 oz.) box
Tomato sauce 1 (8 oz.) can
Cheddar cheese 1 1/2 cups, shredded

Brown onions, garlic and bell pepper in bacon drippings. Add meat and remaining ingredients, except cheese, spaghetti and tomato sauce. Cook sauce until meat is tender. Cook spaghetti. Place spaghetti in 2 quart baking dish; sprinkle with cheese and pour meat sauce over all. Cover meat sauce with tomato sauce. Cover and bake at 350 degrees for 15-20 minutes. Serves 6.

Vodka-Caviar/Blue Corn "Tamale" with Yellow Tomato Pico de Gallo

The Mansion on Turtle Creek - Dallas

Vodka-cured caviar 4 ounces, divide and use
Blue cornmeal crepes 4 (recipe follows)
Leek laces 8, blanched
Jalapeno-corn sour cream 1 cup (recipe follows)
2 tablespoons each of:
Brunoise jalapeno
Red pepper
Red onions
Chopped cilantro
Mexican hard cheese
Yellow tomato pico de gallo 4 tablespoons (recipe follows)

Spoon approximately 1 tablespoon jalapeno sour cream in middle of blue corn crepe. Top with 1/2 ounce vodka caviar. Roll into cylinder. Tie ends with leek laces to resemble a small tamale. Place in center of plate. Nestle yellow tomato pico next to tamale. Sprinkle with 1/2 tablespoon each of the brunoise jalapeno, red pepper, red onions, chopped cilantro and Mexican hard cheese all over plate. Top tamale with remaining 1/2 ounce of caviar. Repeat for other 3 plates and serve. Serves 4.

Blue Cornmeal Crepes

Blue cornmeal 1/4 cup
Flour 1/4 cup
Eggs 2
Milk 1/2 cup
Salt pinch
Sugar pinch

Combine cornmeal and flour. Mix eggs with milk; add salt and sugar. Combine wet and dry ingredients and mix until smooth. Makes 4 thin crepes in non-stick crepe pan.

Leek Laces

Cut white part of leek into 8 1/8 inch thick "laces." Blanch for 1 minute in hot water, then shock in ice cold water.

(continued on next page)

Jalapeno-corn Sour Cream

Jalapeno 1, minced
Shallots 2, minced
Corn puree 2 tablespoons
Cilantro 1 tablespoon, chopped
Lime zest 1 tablespoon
Sour cream 3/4 cup
Salt to taste

Combine all ingredients. Mix well.

Yellow Tomato Pico de Gallo

Yellow tomato 1 large, diced and seeded
Red onion 1, diced
Jalapeno 1, minced
Cilantro 1 tablespoon, chopped
Lime juice 2 tablespoons
Olive oil 1 tablespoon
Salt

Combine all ingredients. Season to taste with salt.

Deanna's East Texas Surprise

Deanna McCarty - Moscow

Ground hamburger 1 pound
Ranch style beans 1 (8 oz.) can
Picante sauce 1/4 cup
Onions 1/2 cup
Chili powder, garlic and **pepper** to taste
Eggs 1-2
Cheese 1 cup, grated

Brown and season hamburger in large skillet. When hamburger is browned, add beans, picante sauce and onion. Add chili powder, garlic and pepper. Let mixture simmer for 5 minutes before adding eggs. Add eggs, stirring until done. Add cheese so it will melt while mixture is still hot. Makes a great hot one-dish meal. No salt is added to cut down on high blood pressure. Serves 5.

Wild Rice & Sausage Stuffed Goose

Barbara Smith - Fort Worth

Goose 1, rinsed and patted dry
Butter 2 tablespoons, melted
Sage 2 teaspoons
Stuffing:
Pork sausage or game sausage 1/2 pound, cooked
Wild rice 3 cups, cooked
Butter 2 tablespoons, melted
Celery 3 stalks, sliced
Onion 1/2 medium, chopped

Mix all stuffing ingredients together in a large bowl. Stir well to combine. Loosely stuff goose. Truss the goose, if desired, and tie the legs together with string. Shield tips of legs with small pieces of foil to prevent overcooking. Mix together the melted butter and sage and brush over the outside of the goose. Insert the temperature probe in the thickest part of the goose, between the legs and the breast. Serves 4-6.

Chicken Broccoli Divan

Ola Marie Robison - Damon

Broccoli 1 pound fresh, cut into spears, cooked and drained
Cooked chicken or turkey 1 1/2 cups, cubed
Pecans 2/3 cup, chopped
Cream of broccoli soup 1 can
Milk 1/3 cup
Cheddar cheese 1/2 cup, shredded
Butter 1 tablespoon
Dry bread crumbs 2 tablespoons

In shallow casserole, arrange broccoli, top with chicken and pecans. Combine soup and milk; pour over chicken. Sprinkle with cheese.

Combine butter and bread crumbs; sprinkle over cheese. Bake at 450 degrees for 15 minutes or until hot. Or cover with wax paper; microwave on High 6 minutes or until hot, rotating dish halfway through heating. Serves 4.

Chicken Breasts, Stuffed with Vegetables and Cheeses

Wild Briar, the Country Inn at Edom - Ben Wheeler

Chicken breast halves 12 with bones removed, skin attached
Onion 1 medium, chopped
Butter 3 tablespoons
Egg yolks 2, beaten
Salt 1/4 teaspoon
Zucchini 4, grated, water removed
Cottage cheese 24 ounce, small curd
Basil 1/2 teaspoon crushed
Parmesan cheese 2 tablespoons grated

Melt butter, add chopped onion, zucchini, cook gently. Add all other ingredients except chicken. Cook just until flavors combine, stirring to mix. Stuff about 1/4 cup of filling under the skin in each chicken breast. Tuck edges of skin to make an attractive serving. Place in buttered baking dish. Place a small pat of butter on the top of each piece of chicken. Bake 350 degrees for 30-35 minutes until golden brown. May be served whole hot or cut into slices and served cold.

Also served as Florentine Chicken by substituting 2 boxes chopped frozen spinach for the zucchini. Thaw and squeeze spinach before adding to butter and onion.

This dish can be prepared early and cooked just after orders are taken to be piping hot as an entree. A little white wine may be added to the baking dish before adding chicken to make a special occasion dish.

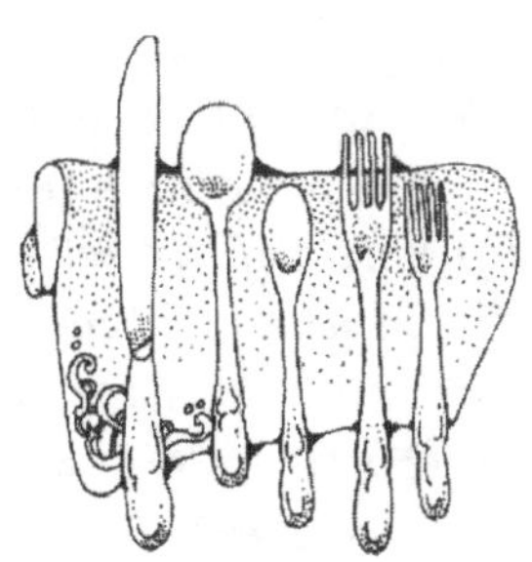

Grilled Wild Boar Chops with Bacon Jalapeno Sauce

Sous Chef William Myers
Y.O. Ranch Hilton - Kerrville

Sauce:

Brown sugar 1 cup
Red wine vinegar 1/2 cup
Beef stock 2 cups
Bacon 3/4 cup, cooked and minced
Jalapenos 4, seeded and minced
Onion 1 tablespoon, minced
Cilantro 1 teaspoon, minced
Black pepper pinch (coarse ground)
Cornstarch 1 tablespoon

Put all ingredients except cornstarch in 2 quart sauce pan and bring to a boil. Mix cornstarch with enough cold water to form a thin paste and add to boiling mixture stirring constantly. Reduce heat and simmer for 15 minutes. May be made 1 or 2 days in advance and refrigerated. Yield approximately 3 cups.

Chops:

Allow 2 one-inch thick chops per person (pork chops may be substituted for wild boar). Place over low heat on BBQ grill. For true Texas results, use mesquite wood. Grill until almost well done. Place on serving platter and drizzle with some hot bacon jalapeno sauce.

Kerrville, in the rugged hill country along the Guadalupe River, is a popular winter and summer resort. Camp Verde, 11 miles south of here, was the eastern terminus of a camel route that started at Ft. Yuma on the Arizona-California border during the 1850s.

South Texas Pork Stir Fry

Carol Barclay - Portland

Oil 1 to 2 tablespoons
Pork tenderloin 1, about 1 1/4 to 1 1/2 pounds, trimmed, thinly sliced and cut into 1/2 inch strips
Chili powder 1 to 2 tablespoons
Green onions 1 bunch, cut into 1 inch pieces
Garlic cloves 2, minced
Black beans 1 (16 oz.) can, drained and rinsed
Cilantro leaves 1 cup
Cherry tomatoes 1 pint, sliced in half
Whole kernel corn 1 cup
Lime juice 1 tablespoon fresh
Salt 1/4 teaspoon
Cooked rice 3 cups

Heat oil in large skillet or wok. Stir fry pork with chili powder until lightly browned. Remove with slotted spoon; set aside. Add onion and garlic to drippings; stir fry 30 seconds. Add rinsed beans, cilantro, cherry tomatoes, corn, lime juice and salt, and stir fry 2 to 3 minutes. Stir in pork; heat through. Serve over hot rice. Not only is this quick but it is a very colorful dish. Serves 6.

Shelia's Cajun Lemon Chops

Shelia Johnson - Houston

Pork or lamb chops 4-6
Wyler's® cajun boullion granules 1 tablespoon
Hot water 1 cup
Lemon juice 2 tablespoons
Dried oregano 1/4 teaspoon
Lemon pepper 1/4 teaspoon
Garlic powder 1/4 teaspoon

Place chops in 6 x 9 baking dish. Combine all other ingredients and pour over the chops. Cook in 350 degree oven for 30 to 45 minutes. Serves 2 to 3.

East Texas Meat Loaf

Vernie Bailey - Kemp

Ground beef 2 pounds
Sesame seed crackers 1 cup, crushed
Onion 1/2 cup, chopped
Green pepper 1/4 cup, chopped
Tomatoes 1 (16 oz.) can
Eggs 2, beaten
Salt 1 1/2 teaspoon
Black pepper 1/2 teaspoon
Basil 1/4 teaspoon

Combine ground beef, cracker crumbs, onion, green pepper, tomatoes, eggs, salt, pepper and basil. Pack mixture into a 9 x 5 loaf pan. Bake in a slow oven (300 degrees) for 2 hours. Serves 8.

Some of the Spanish missions in Texas are older than the ones in California. For example, La Purisima Soccoro Mission, at Ysleta, near El Paso, was built in the 1860s by Piro Indians, a Pueblo tribe. The Indians incorporated Piro symbols into the mission's design.

Sally's Chuckwagon

Sally Walker - Conroe

Ground beef 1 pound
Butter or margarine 3 tablespoons
Tomatoes 1 (15 oz.) can, with liquid, cut tomatoes to bite size
Dark red kidney beans 1 (15 oz.) can, with liquid
Elbow macaroni 3/4 cup
Barbecue sauce 1/2 cup
Worcestershire sauce

Scramble ground beef in butter, add a few shakes of Worcestershire sauce. Drain fat. Add remaining ingredients, simmer 20 minutes, stirring occasionally. Serve with biscuits and cold fruit salad. Serves 6.

Texas Mountain Calf-Fries

Archie Leonard Drain - Denton

Oil or shortening 2 cups
Calf or bull oysters 5 pounds
Salt 1 1/2 tablespoon
Black pepper 1 tablespoon
Beer 2 cans, any kind
Eggs 4, slightly beaten
Yellow corn meal 2 cups

Heat oil or shortening in large skillet. While shortening is heating, slice calf-fries in quarters; salt and pepper. Pour beer into a medium bowl; put calf-fries in beer. Allow to stand for 30 minutes. Dip calf-fries in eggs and roll them in yellow corn meal. Place in skillet of hot shortening and fry to a golden brown. Serves 8.

Tip: Place in a warmer and serve hot.

Beef Brisket

Faye Albertson - Wimberly

Beef brisket 1 (3-5 lb.) boneless, trimmed

Marinate in foil overnight in:
Garlic salt 1 tablespoon
Celery seed 2 tablespoons
Black pepper 1 tablespoon
Accent® 1 tablespoon
Lawry® seasoning salt 1 tablespoon
Liquid Smoke 2 tablespoons
Worcestershire sauce 2 tablespoons

Mix above together. Heat oven to 300 degrees. Cook meat in foil in which it was marinated for 4 hours. Good hot or cold. (Make sure it is sealed tightly in the foil and do not open until ready to eat. This is really foolproof. If using a larger brisket, multiply the marinade ingredients by 1 1/2 or 2.) Serves 8-10.

Cheesy Flounder Fillets

Carol Barclay - Portland

Flounder fillets 1 1/2 pounds
Vegetable coating spray
Yogurt cheese 1/3 cup*
Cornstarch 2 teaspoons
Parmesan cheese 2 tablespoons grated
Parsley 2 tablespoons, fresh if possible
Onion 1/4 cup, minced
Lemon juice 1 tablespoon
Fresh dill 1 tablespoon or 1 teaspoon dried (or use tarragon or marjoram)

Arrange fillets in a 9 x 13 baking pan sprayed with vegetable coating spray. Combine remaining ingredients, spread mixture evenly over fillets. Bake at 350 degrees for 15 minutes or until fish flakes easily. If desired, place under broiler for 1 to 2 minutes until cheese mixture begins to brown. A little red pepper sprinkled over the top before baking is good if you want a little bite. Serves 4-5.

* Note: To make yogurt cheese you will need yogurt that does not contain a stabilizer or gelatin base, and one piece of cheesecloth large enough to fit in a funnel, the finer the cheesecloth the better. Place cloth in funnel and pour in yogurt; place in glass or cup to catch the whey. Refrigerate and allow to drain 8 to 10 hours. You can also buy a yogurt cheese funnel.

Texas Stewed Chicken & Dumplings

Vernie Bailey - Kemp

Stewing hen or chicken 4 pounds

Cut into serving pieces and submerge in large kettle with salted water. Cover, bring to a boil, then reduce flame to simmer and cook until chicken is tender. While chicken is cooking, combine with pastry blender, fork or two knives:

Dumplings:

Flour 1 1/2 cups, sifted
Salt 1/2 teaspoon
Baking powder 1 1/2 teaspoon
Cut in **1/4 cup shortening.**
Add, mixing well:
1/2 cup milk

Turn out onto lightly floured board or pastry cloth and knead lightly. Roll out to 1/8 inch thickness. Cut into strips. When chicken is done and tender, drop strips into the kettle of broth. Cover and continue simmering 20 minutes. Serves 8.

Skillet Chicken & Rice

Chicken breasts 2 whole, deboned, skinned and sliced
Zucchini 1/2 pound, thinly sliced
Broccoli flowerets 1 1/2 - 2 cups
Green onion 1/2 cup chopped
Tomatoes 1 (16 oz.) can, undrained and chopped
Rice 3 cups, cooked, white or brown
Parsley 1/4 cup chopped
Salt 1/2 teaspoon
Pepper 1/4 teaspoon
Dry oregano pinch

Coat large skillet with cooking spray. Sauté chicken till lightly browned. Add zucchini and broccoli; cook until crisp tender. Stir in remaining ingredients. Cover, reduce heat, and simmer 15 minutes or until heated through. Serves 8-10.

Chicken Oriental

Beverly McClatchy - Midland

Fryer 1, cut up
Margarine 1/4 cup
Mushrooms 1 small can, sliced
Pineapple chunks 1 (14 oz.) can
Soy sauce 2 tablespoons
Sugar 2 tablespoons
Vinegar 2 tablespoons
Green peppers 2, cut into strips
Onions 2 medium, sliced
Cornstarch 1 1/2 tablespoons
Cooked rice 3 cups

Cook chicken in margarine until brown. Drain mushrooms and pineapple. Combine liquid of both and add enough water to make 2 cups. Add liquid to chicken, bring to a boil. Reduce heat and cover. Simmer 1 hour. Stir in soy sauce, sugar and vinegar. Add mushrooms, pineapple, peppers and onions. Cook 30 minutes. Blend cornstarch with small amount of water, stir in chicken mixture. Cook until thickened. Serve over rice. Serves 4-6.

Tips: Chicken may be deboned and cut into bite-size pieces. Serve with tossed salad and hot bread.

Creole Chicken Gumbo

Lucy Ozarchuk - Texas City

Flour 2 tablespoons
Oil 4 tablespoons to 1/4 cup
Celery 2 cups, chopped
Onion 1 large
Chicken broth 3 cups
Tomatoes 16-ounce can with juice, chopped
Green pepper 1, chopped
Bay leaf 1
Garlic cloves 2, minced
Okra 2 cups, sliced
Parsley 2 tablespoons, chopped
Salt to taste
Hot pepper sauce 1/4 teaspoon
Shrimp 5-ounce can, drained, or 1 cup fresh shrimp
Chicken 3 cups, cooked
Rice 3 cups, hot cooked

Brown flour in oil to make a roux. Add celery and onion. Cook 10 minutes. Add broth, tomatoes, green pepper, bay leaf, garlic, okra, parsley, salt and pepper sauce. Simmer 45 minutes, stirring occasionally. Add chicken and shrimp. Heat through. Serve in bowls with hot rice. Serves 6.

Texas barbecue is distinctive! The meat of choice is beef, although it can involve pork ribs, venison, chicken or fish. The fuel of choice is mesquite, which gives the meat its delightfully-smoky flavor. Some food companies even bottle a liquid mesquite smoke for use when the famous desert wood is not available. Preparation of the meat for a Texas barbecue is a process involving dry rubbing and mopping. The rub is a mixture of salt, pepper, herbs and spices. Mopping uses dish mops for basting the meat with "secret" sauces.

Classic Barbecue Sauce

Reprinted from *Best Barbecue Recipes**

Vegetable oil 1/2 cup
Vinegar 1/4 cup
Worcestershire sauce 1/4 cup
Tomato sauce 8-ounce can
Onion 2 1/2 tablespoons, minced
Brown sugar 2 tablespoons
Chili powder 1 tablespoon
Sugar 1 teaspoon
Seasoned salt 1/2 teaspoon

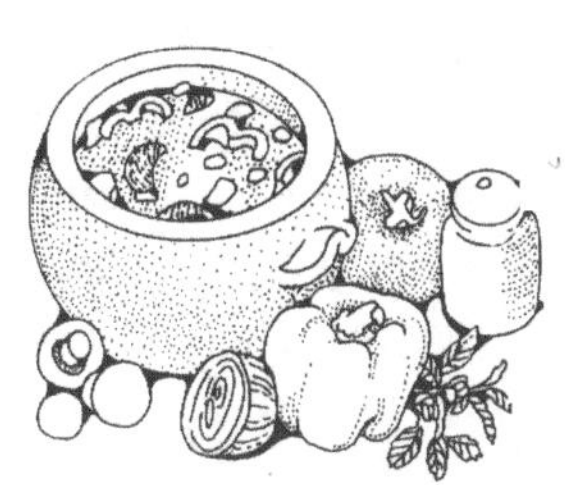

Combine all ingredients. Let stand five minutes. Stir before using to brush on chicken or turkey parts. Serve with remaining sauce. Makes 2 cups.

*Published by Golden West Publishers

Texas Tornado Barbecue Chicken

Utopia on the River - Utopia

Chickens 2, whole
Beer 2 cans

Texas Dust

Iodized salt 2 teaspoons
Black pepper 1/2 teaspoon
Chili powder 3/4 teaspoon
Garlic powder 3/4 teaspoon
Celery salt 3/4 teaspoon
Red pepper 3/4 teaspoon
Onion salt 3/4 teaspoon
Accent® 1/2 teaspoon

Mix all ingredients together and rub onto chicken. Wash and dry chickens. Rub Texas Dust onto chickens. Place whole chickens over full cans of opened beers, so that chickens cover the whole cans. Place chickens and beers upright on grill. Close grill door and let warm beers steam your chickens while you have a cold one. Serves 4-8.

The history of the Texas Tornado Barbecue is older than the barbecue itself. It hearkens to a time when the good things in life, like an occasional beer, were looked down upon. It was a time when such things as beer sipping were unlawful. Poor cooks were left to their own devices to try and hide their vices, but their hiding places—such as worn-out boots, the barn (behind the wood-burning furnace), and grandma's sewing bag—were soon found out.

But the cooks, crafty souls that they were, discovered the very food they were preparing was a darn good place for hiding vices. Old Jake Hatman's cornbread recipe for hiding cigarettes wasn't too successful, even though it gave another meaning to chewing tobacco.

Seems this cook who discovered and created the Texas Tornado Barbecue had the same idea when she tried hiding a can of beer in a whole chicken.

Though the idea hasn't fully caught on in this dry precinct in the Texas Hill Country, it's a beer drinker's and chicken lover's dream.

Grandma's Old Fashion Barbecue Sauce

Reprinted from *Best Barbecue Recipes*

Onions 6 large, diced
Cooking oil 8-ounce bottle
Tomato sauce 6 (8 oz.) cans
Butter 1 stick, 1/4 pound
Mustard 2 teaspoons, prepared
Mayonnaise 1 1/2 tablespoon
Ketchup 14-ounce bottle
Barbecue sauce 18-ounce bottle
Tabasco® sauce 25-30 drops
Sugar 3 cups

Heat cooking oil and add onions until smothered. Next, add tomato sauce and let simmer three minutes. Then add remaining ingredients except sugar. Let mixture cook five minutes, then add sugar gradually, stirring constantly. Lower heat and cook (covered) slowly, about 1-2 hours. Sauce can also be used over spaghetti.

Although some parts of the country, when barbecuing meat on an outdoor grill rotisserie or pit, use such woods as hickory or oak, most of Texas and the Southwestern United States use mesquite (mes-keet). Mesquite, a small native desert tree, grows wild in the desert and chaparral areas of the Southwest and Mexico. Burning aromatic mesquite logs or charcoal produces a smoke that lends a distinctive and appetizing flavor to beef, ribs and varieties of meat, fish, poultry and vegetables.

Lubbock's Favorite BBQ Sauce

Oil 2 tablespoons
Onion 1, chopped
Ketchup 1 cup
Water 1/2 cup
Brown sugar 1/4 cup
Worcestershire sauce 3 tablespoons
Salt 1 tablespoon
Garlic powder 1/4 teaspoon

Heat oil in saucepan and sauté onion until tender. Add remaining ingredients, stir and simmer covered for about 8-10 minutes. Makes 2 cups sauce.

Lubbock, in the South Plains region is one of the main agricultural centers of Texas. The city ships livestock, grain and cotton. It was named for Col. Thomas Lubbock, a Confederate officer and brother of a Texas governor.

Barbecue Sauce with Mushrooms

Reprinted from *Best Barbecue Recipes*

Onion 3/4 cup
Celery 3/4 cup
Mushrooms 1/2 cup
Oil 1/4 cup
Brown sugar 1/2 cup
Mustard 1 tablespoon plus 1 teaspoon, prepared
Salt 1 teaspoon
Worcestershire sauce 1 tablespoon plus 1 teaspoon
Cider vinegar 2 tablespoons
Water 1 1/4 cups

Mince onions, celery and mushrooms. Heat oil in a saucepan. Add minced vegetables and sauté without browning. Add remaining ingredients, stir and simmer for 30 minutes. Stir occasionally, or until thickened. Makes 1 quart of sauce.

Golden Grill Barbecue Sauce

Reprinted from *Best Barbecue Recipes*

Sugar 1/4 cup
Cornstarch 2 tablespoons
Allspice 1/2 teaspoon
Cloves 1/2 teaspoon, ground
Orange juice 1 cup, fresh
Vinegar 2 tablespoons
Butter or margarine 4 tablespoons

Combine sugar, cornstarch, allspice and cloves in a small saucepan. Slowly stir in orange juice and vinegar. Stir constantly over medium heat until sauce thickens. Boil for 3 minutes. Stir in butter. Makes 1 cup sauce.

Barbecue Sauce

Reprinted from *Best Barbecue Recipes*

Tomato ketchup 1 cup
Cider vinegar 1/2 cup
Sugar 1 teaspoon
Chili powder 1 teaspoon
Salt 1/8 teaspoon
Water 1 1/2 cups
Celery 3 stalks, chopped
Bay leaves 3
Garlic 1 clove
Onion 2 tablespoons chopped
Butter 4 tablespoons
Worcestershire sauce 4 tablespoons
Paprika 1 teaspoon
Black pepper dash

Combine all ingredients and bring to a boil. Simmer about 15 minutes. Remove from heat and strain. This is a table sauce to be served with beef, chicken or pork. Do not cook things in it. Makes about 2 1/2 cups sauce.

Comfort Bar-B-Que Sauce

Margarine 3 tablespoons
Onions 1/2 cup, diced
Tomato puree 1 cup
Worcestershire sauce 3 tablespoons
Ketchup 1 1/3 cups
Steak Sauce 3 tablespoons
Vinegar 1 tablespoon
Lemon juice 1 teaspoon
Liquid Smoke 2 tablespoons
Soy sauce 1 1/2 teaspoon
Dry mustard 3/4 teaspoon
Honey 2 tablespoons
Brown sugar 2 tablespoons
Accent® 1 teaspoon
Salt 1 1/2 teaspoon
Chili powder 1/2 to 1 teaspoon
Hot water 4 cups
Black pepper scant

Melt margarine and sauté onions. Add remaining ingredients and mix. Simmer one hour or longer until sauce is of desired consistency. Sauce may be frozen at this point. Makes 6 cups.

Note: To thicken sauce quickly, add 2 tablespoons cornstarch to 2 cups cold water. Add to sauce and cook until sauce thickens. Do not freeze after cornstarch has been added.

Comfort was settled by free-thinking, non-religious German immigrants. Trekking from Indianola, Texas, some of the travelers settled at Round Top; others continued to what is now New Braunfels. Still others migrated to what they considered a "comfortable" area at the junction of Cypress Creek and Guadalupe River. The town name was shortened to Comfort when a post office was established there in 1856.

Barbecued Corn-on-the-Cob

Reprinted from *Best Barbecue Recipes*

Strip husks down to end of cob, but do not remove. Tear off silk threads. Allow husked corn to stand in cold, salted water for 10 minutes. Brush corn with softened butter or margarine and season with salt and pepper. Bring husks back up around cob, making sure entire ear is covered. Secure husks with picture-hanging wire or strip of corn husk tied tightly.

Place ears in double thickness of heavy-duty aluminum foil, twisting foil ends securely. Place on briquets for about 10 minutes, turning once.

When corn is done, remove wire and husks and serve immediately.

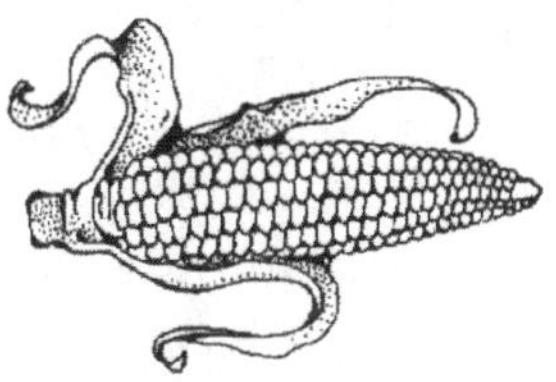

Seasoned Butters for Corn-on-the-Cob

Combine 1/2 cup (1 stick) **butter** (softened) with one of the following:
1/2 teaspoon **curry powder or chili powder**, or
1/2 teaspoon **hickory smoked salt**, or
1 teaspoon **chopped chives or parsley**, or
1 teaspoon **herb seasoning** (finely ground).

Makes enough seasoned butter for 6-8 ears of corn.

Fruit Kabobs with Whiskey Baste

Courtesy The Kingsford Company

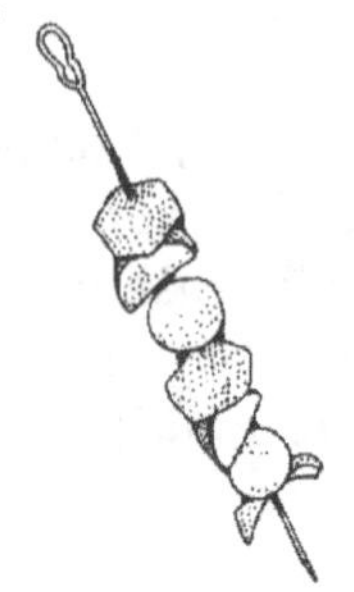

Honey 2 tablespoons
Whiskey 2 tablespoons
Lemon juice 1 tablespoon
Pineapple chunks 8-ounce can, drained
Banana 1 large, bias sliced into 1-inch pieces
Orange 1, peeled and sectioned
Maraschino cherries 8
Skewers 4, 12-inch, bamboo or metal

In a mixing bowl combine the honey, whiskey and lemon juice. Add pineapple chunks, banana pieces, orange sections and cherries. Gently toss to coat fruit well. Cover and refrigerate up to 2 hours until ready to grill.

Remove fruit with slotted spoon, reserving the whiskey baste to brush on fruit kabobs while grilling.

Alternately thread the fruit onto skewers. Grill the fruit kabobs on a covered grill, directly over moderately-low Kingsford® briquets for 5-10 minutes or until fruit is warmed through. Serves 4.

Note: If bamboo skewers are used, soak them in water for 20 minutes before using on the grill.

All Purpose Game Marinade

Barbara Smith - Fort Worth

Oil 1/2 cup
White vinegar 1 1/2 cups
Liquid Smoke 1/4 teaspoon
Bay leaf 1
Salt 1/2 teaspoon
Worcestershire sauce 6 tablespoons
Pepper corns 1 teaspoon

Combine all ingredients. Refrigerate well before using. Good for dry cuts of game such as flank steaks, small game with little fat or round steaks. Yield: 2 cups.

Side Dishes

Stir-Fry Brown Rice

Texmati Brands Rice Products - Alvin

Bacon 6 slices chopped
Onions 1/2 cup chopped
Chicken 1 1/2 pounds boned and skinned, cut into strips
Mushrooms 1 (4 oz.) can sliced, drained
Snow peas 1 cup
Texmati® Brown rice 3 cups cooked
Pimentos 1/4 cup diced
Salt 1 1/4 teaspoons
Pepper 1 teaspoon
Soy sauce 1 tablespoon

In large skillet, fry bacon and onions until transparent. Add chicken and cook 5-10 minutes until chicken is slightly browned. Stir in remaining ingredients. Heat thoroughly. Serves 6.

The Alamo became the cradle of Texas liberty when its 187 defenders valiantly fought to the last man, defending the fort against the 5,000-soldier Mexican army under Gen. Santa Ana. This heroism bought time for Sam Houston's troops and inspired the cry "Remember the Alamo!"

Tomato Pie

Adele Tibbs - Big Spring

This recipe was the Grand Champion at the Martin County Fair.

Unbaked pie crust 1, 9 inch
Tomatoes 3 large, sliced
Salt and pepper to taste
Oregano 1/2 to 1 teaspoon
Green onion 1 cup, chopped
Cheddar cheese 2 cups, sharp grated
Mayonnaise 1 cup
Parmesan cheese 1/2 cup, grated

Preheat oven to 400 degrees. Prick crust with a fork and bake for 10 minutes. Remove from oven and reduce heat to 325 degrees. Cover pie crust with 2 layers of tomatoes. Sprinkle with salt and pepper and half the oregano and onions. Repeat layers. Combine cheddar cheese and mayonnaise and spread over pie. Top with parmesan. Bake for 45 minutes.

Western Limas and Ham Hock

Vernie Bailey - Kemp

Lima beans 2 cups large
Ham hock 1 small
Water 5 cups
Chopped onion 3/4 cup
Pepper 1/8 teaspoon
Salt to taste

Sort and wash lima beans, drain, combine ingredients; bring to a boil. Reduce heat. Simmer 2 1/2 to 3 hours or until ham and beans are tender. Remove bone from ham, cut meat into pieces, and return to beans. Heat a few minutes before serving. Serves 4-6.

Rattlesnake Corn Relish

Executive Chef John Billings
Y. O. Ranch Hilton - Kerrville

Cut corn 2 pounds, frozen
Rattlesnake 2 pounds, cooked, diced
Tomatoes 4 medium, diced
Jalapenos 4, diced
Red onion 1, diced
Green onions 6, sliced
Cilantro 1 bunch, chopped
Black pepper 1 tablespoon
Salt 1 tablespoon

Mix all ingredients together and chill for 1 hour.

Squash Casserole

Bonnie Dixon - Alvarado

Yellow squash 1 pound
Onion 1 small, chopped
Salt 1 teaspoon
Pepper 1/2 teaspoon
Egg 1
Saltine crackers 8, crumbled
Cheese 1 cup, grated
Margarine 2 tablespoons

In small amount of boiling water, cook squash and onion till tender. Drain. Mash a little and add salt, pepper, egg, crackers, cheese and margarine. Beat all together and place in buttered casserole. Bake 350 degrees 30 minutes. (For an attractive contrast use 1/2 yellow squash and 1/2 zucchini.) Serves 4.

East Texas Onion Pudding

The Mansion on Turtle Creek - Dallas

Peanut oil 3 tablespoons
Yellow onions 4 medium to large, peeled and sliced
Heavy cream 1 cup
Whole eggs 4 large
Garlic cloves 2, peeled and minced
Cayenne pepper, salt and lemon juice to taste
Tobacco onions (see page 101)

Preheat oven to 300 degrees. Heat oil in a large sauté pan over medium heat. Add onions and sauté for 10-12 minutes until completely transparent but not brown. Remove from heat and cool until they can be handled. In a medium size mixing bowl, add cream, eggs, garlic and whip together. Add onions and season with cayenne, salt and lemon juice. Pour into a small 8 inch ceramic dish and place on center rack of the oven. Cook for approximately 20 minutes or until top begins to set. Sprinkle tobacco onions evenly over the pudding and return to oven until center is completely set, about 15 minutes. Cover loosely with aluminum foil if onions begin to get too brown. Remove pudding from oven when done and allow to rest for 10 minutes prior to serving.

The Mansion on Turtle Creek in Dallas includes the original Sheppard King Mansion, constructed in 1925, and an adjacent hotel. A restaurant, additional dining rooms and meeting rooms, and multi-purpose rooms are all designed to complement the lavish style of the original mansion.

Tobacco Onions

Peanut oil 3 cups (or other light oil for frying)
Yellow or sweet onions 2 large, peeled and sliced very thin (about 1/8 in.)
All-purpose flour 1 cup
Salt 1 teaspoon
Black pepper 1 teaspoon
Cayenne pepper 1/2 teaspoon
Paprika 1 teaspoon

Heat oil over moderate heat. Combine all other ingredients and toss well. Remove onion slices from flour mixture, tossing to remove excess. Fry in hot oil until crisp and golden brown, about 2 minutes.

Mango-Corn Relish

The Mansion on Turtle Creek - Dallas

Corn 2 ears
Mango 1, peeled and cut into small dice
Red onion 2 tablespoons, finely diced
Red bell pepper 2 tablespoons, finely diced
Cilantro 1 tablespoon, finely chopped
Lime juice 1 teaspoon
Maple syrup 1 teaspoon
Salt to taste

Roast whole ears (shucks on) on a cookie sheet in a 350 degree oven for 20 minutes. Remove and allow to cool. Shuck and remove silk. Cut kernels from cob, avoiding the chewy heart alongside the cob. Place corn in a medium mixing bowl with all other ingredients. Mix well, and let stand 1 hour before serving.

Autumn Squash Relish

The Mansion on Turtle Creek - Dallas
Chef Randall Warder

Water 2 cups
Salt 1 teaspoon
Acorn squash 2/3 cup, peeled and cut into medium dice, about 1/2" cubes
Celery 1/3 cup, peeled and cut into medium dice as above
Red bell pepper 1/3 cup, cut into medium dice as above
Orange peel 1 teaspoon, finely grated
Sage 1 teaspoon, chopped
Thyme 1 teaspoon, chopped
Lemon juice 2 teaspoons
Salt and cayenne pepper to taste

Place water in a small sauce pan. Add salt and bring to a boil. Add diced acorn squash and cook until softened but not falling apart, about 2 minutes. Strain squash and place under cool running water for 20 seconds to stop cooking. In a small mixing bowl, combine the squash, celery, bell pepper, orange peel, herbs and lemon juice. Season to taste with salt and cayenne pepper.

Presentation:

Ladle 3 teaspoons sauce in the center of each heated plate. Place 1 chop on each plate, and behind the bone spoon some of the East Texas Onion Pudding. Garnish the other side with one or two tablespoons of the Autumn Squash Relish. Serve immediately.

Once known as "The Wall Street of the Southwest," the Strand District of Galveston, with its Victorian buildings, has been restored to its 19th-century splendor. The area is noted for its iron-fronted buildings, one of the nation's best-known collection of such architecture.

Sautéed Sweet Peppers

Ralph W. Wagnon - Seguin

Bell peppers 3
Canola oil or meat drippings 2 tablespoons
Soy sauce 1/2 cup
Honey 1/2 cup
Canola or olive oil 1 tablespoon

Dice bell peppers and sauté in 2 tablespoons of canola oil or meat drippings until tender crisp. In a small bowl combine soy sauce, honey and 1 tablespoon canola or olive oil. Pour over peppers and stir to coat well. Continue cooking until peppers are done to your taste. Serves 4.

Tip: Try using 1 red, 1 yellow and 1 green bell pepper for color. Great served over steak or roast or as a side dish.

Shauna's Potatoes

Faye Albertson (for Shauna Loy) - Wimberley

Butter 1/2 cup, melted
Onions 1/2 cup, grated or chopped
Frozen hash browns 32 ounce package, sightly thawed
Sour cream 16 ounces
Cream of mushroom soup 2 cans
Cheddar cheese 2 cups, grated
Salt and pepper to taste

Sauté onions in butter till tender. Mix all ingredients together and spread in greased 9 x 12 casserole dish. Bake at 350 degrees for 1 to 1 1/2 hours or until bubbly and slightly browned. Serves 10-12.

South Texas Sweet Onion Rings

Carol Barclay - Portland

Buttermilk 1/3 cup
Jalapenos 3, chopped with seeds
Onion 1 large, cut into 1/4 inch thick rings
Vegetable oil 6 cups
Flour 2 cups
Salt

Mix buttermilk and jalapenos in a blender until only small flecks of pepper remain. Pour into large bowl. Add onion rings and toss well. Cover and let stand at room temperature at least 4 to 5 hours.

Heat oil in frying pan to 325 degrees. Drain raw onion rings in colander, shaking well. Dredge rings thoroughly in flour; do not shake off excess. In small batches, fry rings in hot oil until golden brown, about 3 minutes. Transfer rings to a large baking sheet covered with a triple thickness of paper towels to absorb excess grease. Sprinkle with salt. Serve immediately. Serves 4.

Okra and Rice Fritters

Enell Helen Creel - Texas City

Okra 1 1/2 cups, chopped
Rice 1 1/2 cups, cooked
Tomatoes 1 cup, chopped
Onions 3/4 cup, chopped
Salt 1 1/2 teaspoon
Pepper 3/4 teaspoon
Baking powder 1 teaspoon
Sugar 1 tablespoon
Cornmeal 1 cup
Flour 1 cup
Eggs 2, beaten
Oil for deep frying

Mix first 8 ingredients. Mix flour and cornmeal. Pour the beaten eggs over the okra mixture and combine. Add the meal and flour mixture and stir together. Drop the batter by tablespoons into hot oil. Cook until well-browned, turn as needed. Serves 8.

Chili Cheese Tomatoes

Carol Barclay - Portland

Tomatoes 3 large or 4 medium (firm)
Sour cream 1 cup
Salt 1/2 teaspoon
Pepper 1/4 teaspoon
Flour 1 tablespoon
Green onions 2 tablespoons, chopped
Green chiles 1 small can, chopped
Cheddar cheese 1 cup, grated

Slice tomatoes and cut in thick slices. Mix remaining ingredients in a small bowl and stir until well blended. Place tomato slices in a broiler pan or shallow glass baking dish. Spoon sour cream mixture evenly over tomato slices. Top with extra grated cheese if desired. This may be done early in the day and refrigerated. Just before serving, broil tomatoes about 4 minutes or until cheese is bubbly or top is golden brown. The tomatoes will be just warm. These will warm over nicely the next day if you have any left. Serves 8.

Tip: These tomatoes are not only good with any meat but very good served for a brunch.

Home of dinosaurs more than 100 million years ago, Dinosaur Flats, near New Braunfels, is the world's largest area of dinosaur tracks. Since they were discovered in 1982, hundreds of tracks have been uncovered on a hillside near Canyon Lake.

Larry's Crossing Hobo Beans

Barbara Smith - Fort Worth

Brown sugar 1 cup
Sugar 1 cup
Barbecue sauce 1/2 cup
Ketcup 1/2 cup
Mustard 1/4 cup
Bacon 1/2 cup, cooked and finely chopped
Salt 1/2 tablespoon
Worcestershire sauce 1 tablespoon
Tabasco® sauce 1/2 tablespoon
Louisiana hot sauce (or additional tabasco) 1/2 tablespoon
Water 1/2 cup
Pork 'n beans 64 ounce can

Combine ingredients and simmer for 30 minutes.

Tip: If you would like to make authentic hobo beans, add a half pound Larry's Crossing® Chopped barbecue. As an alternative, add 1/2 pound browned ground beef.

Candied Sweet Potatoes

JoAnn Tucker - Chico

Sweet potatoes 3 large
Sugar 2/3 cup
Water 1/3 cup
Butter 2 tablespoons
Orange juice 3 tablespoons

Preheat oven to 400 degrees. Scrub potatoes to remove dirt. Boil in water until tender. Peel and cut in half lengthwise and place in buttered dish. Make syrup by boiling sugar, water, butter and orange juice. Pour over potatoes. Bake for 25-30 minutes, basting once or twice with syrup while baking. Serves 4.

Texas Baked Corn

Pat Stone - Conroe

Whole kernel corn 1 can, drained
Creamed style corn 2 cans
Sugar 3 tablespoons
Flour 3 tablespoons
Eggs 4, beaten
Onion 1/2 to 1 small (to taste), chopped
Bell pepper 1/2 to 1 (to taste), chopped
Margarine 1/2 stick, melted
Salt 1/4 teaspoon
Black pepper 1/2 teaspoon
Red pepper 1/4 teaspoon

Combine all ingredients and pour into a greased uncovered baking dish (approximately 9 x 9 or round casserole dish). Bake at 400 degrees 45-60 minutes until center is firm. Serves 8.

Variation: Use whole kernel Mexican corn for a Mexican food dish.

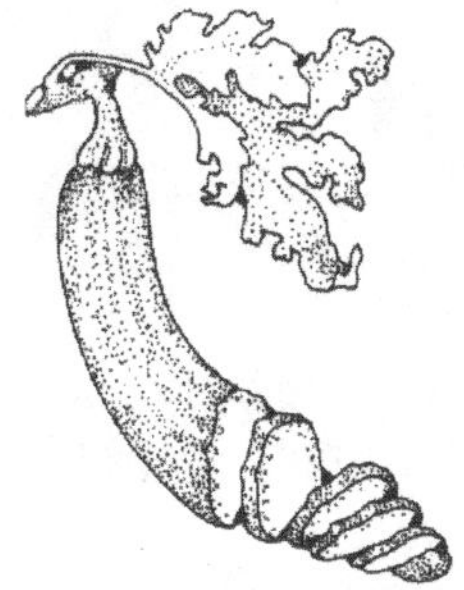

Zucchini Casserole

Beverly McClatchy - Midland

Zucchini 4 medium size, sliced
Onion 1 medium, sliced
Cheez Whiz® 1 (16 oz.) jar
Green chiles 1 (7 oz.) can

Line casserole dish with zucchini. Spread onions on top. Add green chiles and spoon on Cheez Whiz. Cover with foil. Bake 350 degrees until zucchini is tender, about 45 minutes. Check tenderness with fork. Serves 6.

San Jacinto Sweet Potato Casserole

Imperial Sugar Company - Sugar Land

Sweet potatoes 3 cups (1 lb. 14 oz.), drained and mashed
Brown sugar 1/4 cup, packed
Salt 1/2 teaspoon
Cinnamon 1/2 teaspoon
Egg 1, beaten
Milk 1/2 cup
Mandarin orange sections 1 can (11 oz.), drained, or 1 cup fresh orange sections or pineapple chunks
Miniature marshmallows 1 1/2 cups, divided

Combine all ingredients except fruit and marshmallows; whip until light and fluffy. Fold in fruit and half of marshmallows. Spoon into individual baking dishes or a 6-cup baking dish. Bake at 350 degrees for about 20 minutes. Top with remaining marshmallows and return to oven until marshmallows are light brown and beginning to melt. Serves 8.

Squash Dressing

Barbara Smith - Fort Worth

Cornbread mix 1 package
Squash 1 1/2 cup, cooked
Butter 2 tablespoons
Sugar 2 tablespoons
Salt 1 teaspoon
Eggs 2
Onion 1, small, finely chopped
Bell pepper 1, finely chopped
Pimento 1 jar
Velveeta® cheese 1/2 pound, cubed
Cream of mushroom soup 1 can

Bake cornbread (I use Jalapeno) according to directions. Cook squash till tender. Season with butter, sugar, salt. Beat eggs, add to cornbread and squash. Sauté onion and bell pepper till tender; add with pimento. Cube cheese and add to mixture along with mushroom soup. Bake in a casserole dish at 375 degrees until brown.

Baked Squash Casserole

Sue Nutt - Arlington

Yellow squash 2 pounds
Margarine 1 stick, melted
Eggs 2, beaten
Milk 2 tablespoons
Instant minced onion 2 tablespoons
Salt 1 teaspoon
Pepper to taste
Ritz® cracker crumbs 2 cups (reserve 1/2 cup for topping)
Cheddar cheese 1 1/2 cups, grated (reserve 1/2 cup for topping)

Slice squash and cook in a pan of water until tender. Drain and mash the squash. Stir in the rest of the ingredients. Pour into large greased baking dish. Top with 1/2 cup Ritz® cracker crumbs and 1/2 cup grated cheddar cheese. Bake at 375 degrees for 45 minutes. Serves 8.

"Guy Texas" Glorified Cabbage

Ola Marie Robison - Damon

Cook **one large head of cabbage**, shredded, until tender. Use small amount of salt and pepper.

Sauce:

Margarine 1 stick
Onion 1 large, chopped
Cream of mushroom soup 1 can
Cheese 1/2 pound
Bread crumbs

Cook onions in melted margarine until clear. Add soup, undiluted. Add cheese. Stir until smooth. Add cabbage and mix well. Pour into casserole and top with bread crumbs. Bake at 350 degrees until bubbly and crumbs are slightly brown.

Piney Woods Hush Puppies

Imperial Sugar Company - Sugar Land

Yellow corn meal 2 1/2 cups
Baking soda 1 teaspoon
Salt 1 teaspoon
Sugar 2 tablespoons
All-purpose flour 2 tablespoons
Baking powder 1 tablespoon
Egg 1, beaten
Buttermilk 2 cups
Cooking oil 1 1/2 cups

Mix all dry ingredients; beat milk and egg together and combine with dry ingredients; batter should hold its shape when picked up in spoon. If it is too soft, add more cornmeal. Drop by rounded tablespoonful into 350 degree oil and cook about 1 1/2 minutes; turn and cook on second side 1 minute. Allow oil to heat a few seconds after removing a batch. Delicious freshly cooked and hot; however, leftover hush puppies freeze well. When ready to serve frozen hush puppies, place on oven rack in preheated 250 degree oven until very hot and crisp. Makes about 48 hush puppies 2" round.

Hints on frying: Using a small diameter heavy sauce pan allows using a minimum of oil; a 5 or 6 inch pan with oil 1 1/2 inches deep and heated to 350 degrees will cook three hush puppies in about 2 1/2 minutes. When batter consistency is correct and oil is at 350 degrees, hush puppies will become firm, round shapes almost as soon as they enter the hot oil. If they are cooked in oil that is too hot, they will not cook in the center.

Serving suggestion: Especially good served with fried catfish, trout, shrimp, oysters, chicken or chicken-fried steak.

The Astrodome, in Houston, is the world prototype domed stadium. Seating up to 76,000, it's used by the Astros, the Oilers and the University of Houston Cougars. Annual special events include the Bluebonnet Bowl in December and the International Livestock Show and Rodeo in February.

Judge Roy Beans

Imperial Sugar Company - Sugar Land

The judge's prisoners wanted to stay in jail for these beans.

Sugar 1/2 cup
Vinegar 1/2 cup
Water 1 cup
Mixed pickling spices 1 teaspoon
Whole green beans 1 (1 lb.) can, drained
Onion 1 small, thinly sliced

Combine sugar, vinegar, water and spices in sauce pan and bring to boil; simmer 10 minutes over lowered heat. Strain vinegar mixture over beans and onions. Cover and chill 24 hours. Serves 4.

Note: Oftentimes, the flavors of frequently served vegetables become overly familiar. That's when skillful use of herbs and spices can make a delightful difference. This recipe is a good example. Vinegar and pickling spices are used to accent the taste of green beans.

The Judge Roy Bean Visitor Center in Langtry boasts the Jersey Lilly, a saloon named for Lillie Langtry, where the judge dispensed beer, whiskey and "the law west of the Pecos."

Squash Dressing

Enell Helen Creel - Texas City

Gooseneck yellow squash 2 cups
Margarine 1/2 stick
Onion 1 large, chopped
Cornbread 2 cups, crumbled
Cream of chicken soup 1 can
Salt and pepper to taste

Combine all ingredients in casserole dish. Bake 30-40 minutes at 400 degrees uncovered. Serves 6.

Asparagus Milanese

Nena Robinson - La Marque

Asparagus 24, fresh, thin
Egg 1
Italian style bread crumbs 1/2 cup, dry
Parmesan cheese 1/3 cup, grated
Vegetable oil 1/2 cup
Salt to taste

Trim bottom of asparagus leaving a stalk about 5 inches long. Beat egg lightly in large flat soup plate. Combine bread crumbs and cheese, spread on large plate. Dip asparagus in egg, then gently roll in crumbs, coating each stalk well. Heat oil in large skillet over high heat. Fry asparagus until lightly crisp and golden. Drain on paper towel. Add salt and serve promptly. Serves 4-6.

Vegetable Rice Casserole

Lee Lambert - Santa Fe

Converted white rice 4 ounces
Carrots 1 cup, sliced
Instant vegetable broth mix 1 packet
Zucchini 1 cup, sliced
Yellow squash 1 cup, sliced
Celery 1 cup, sliced
Leeks 1/2 cup, sliced
Parsley 2 tablespoons, chopped fresh
Oregano 1/4 teaspoon, dried
White pepper 1/8 teaspoon
Monterey jack cheese 5 ounces, coarsely grated

Place rice, carrots, broth mix and 1 1/2 cups water into 2 quart microwave-safe casserole. Cover and vent. Microwave on high 4 minutes, until boiling. Stir. Cover and microwave on medium 10 minutes. Stir in remaining ingredients except cheese. Cover and cook on medium 10 minutes, until rice and vegetables are tender. Stir in cheese. Let stand 5 minutes. Serves 4.

Harvest Baked Acorn Squash

Larry Eason - Texas City

Acorn squash 3 large
Water 1 cup
Pineapple tidbits 13 1/2-ounce can
Red apples 1 1/2 cups, diced, unpeeled
Celery 1 cup, chopped
Walnuts 1/2 cup, chopped
Butter 1/4 cup
Brown sugar 1/2 cup
Cinnamon 1/2 teaspoon
Salt 1/4 teaspoon

Cut squash in halves. Scoop out seeds. Place cut side down in large glass baking dish. Add 1 cup water to bottom of dish. Bake at 350 degrees for 45 minutes. Meanwhile, combine pineapple, apples, celery and walnuts in a small bowl. Melt butter and blend in sugar, cinnamon and salt. Pour this mixture over pineapple mixture, tossing lightly. Remove squash from oven. Drain off water and turn cut side up. Spoon pineapple mixture into squash. Return to oven and bake 15-20 minutes longer, until squash is tender. Serves 6.

Zippy Squash

Texas City Sun - Santa Fe

Yellow squash 1 1/2 pounds
Cooking spray
Onion 1 large, chopped
Salt and pepper to taste
Paprika 1/8 teaspoon (optional)
Green chiles 4-ounce can, mild
Longhorn cheddar cheese 1 cup, grated

Preheat oven to 350 degrees. Slice squash thinly. Microwave about 6 minutes or boil in pan until just crunchy-tender (not overboiled and soft). Coat skillet with cooking spray and sauté onions until just softened, but still crunchy. Lightly spray 1 1/2 quart baking dish. Layer 1/2 of the ingredients in the following order: onions, drained squash, salt, pepper and paprika, green chiles and cheese. Repeat the layers in this order, ending with the cheese. Bake uncovered for 15 minutes. Serves 6.

Watermelon Cake

Carol Barclay - Portland

White cake mix 1 box
Gelatin 1 (3 oz.) package mixed fruit
Watermelon cubes 1 1/3 cups, seedless
Egg whites 3
Oil 1 tablespoon

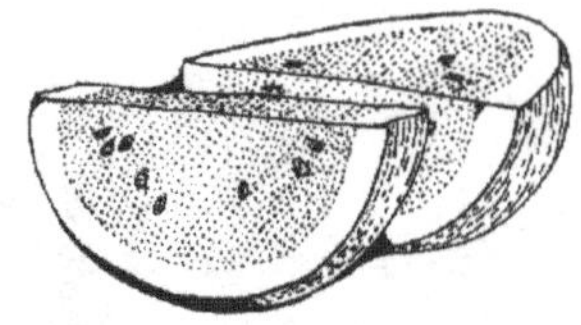

Preheat oven to 350 degrees. Grease and flour bundt pan or spray with cooking spray. In a large bowl, mix all ingredients. Pour into bundt pan and bake about 35 minutes or until wooden pick inserted in cake comes out clean. Invert on serving plate. When cool, ice with watermelon icing. Serves 16.

Icing:

Cream cheese 2 (3 oz.) packages
Butter 1/4 cup
Powdered sugar 2 cups
Watermelon juice 1/4 cup

In a bowl, mix cream cheese and butter until fluffy. Add powdered sugar and watermelon juice; stir until blended. Spread on cool cake.

Puttin' on the Peach Cake

Carol Barclay - Portland

Peach puree 2 cups, fresh (about 5 medium peaches, peeled, pitted and sliced)
Butter 1/2 cup
Sugar 1 cup
Eggs 3, lightly beaten
All-purpose flour 2 cups, sifted
Baking powder 1 teaspoon
Cinnamon 1/2 teaspoon
Baking soda 1 teaspoon
Salt 1/4 teaspoon
Vanilla 1 teaspoon
Pecans 1/2 cup, chopped

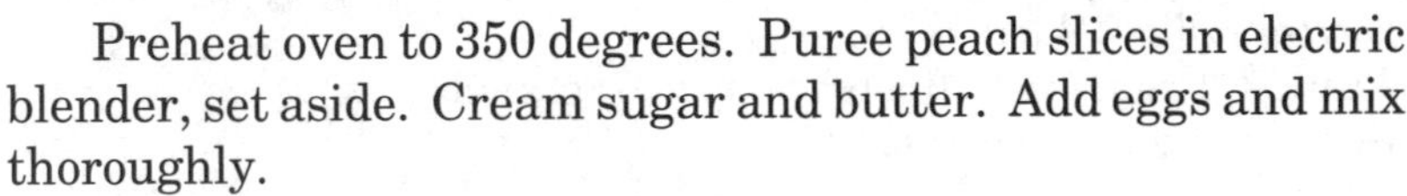

Preheat oven to 350 degrees. Puree peach slices in electric blender, set aside. Cream sugar and butter. Add eggs and mix thoroughly.

Sift together flour, baking powder, baking soda, salt and cinnamon. Add peach puree and dry ingredients alternately to egg mixture, beating well after each addition. Add vanilla and pecans. Mix well. Spoon batter into well greased floured fluted tube pan and bake 30-40 minutes or until cake begins to pull away from side of pan. Do not overbake. Invert on serving plate and let stand to cool. Serve with warmed peach sauce.

Peach Sauce:

Sugar 3/4 cup
Cornstarch 3 tablespoons
Salt 1/4 teaspoon
Peaches 3 cups peeled, sliced (about 4 medium)
Water 1 1/2 cups
Butter 3 tablespoons
Orange flavored liqueur 6 tablespoons

Combine sugar, cornstarch and salt in sauce pan. Add sliced peaches and water. Cook, stirring often, until thick. Add butter and liqueur. Store in refrigerator and heat gently before serving. Cake with sauce will serve approx. 20.

Fresh Apple Pound Cake

Adams Extract Company - Austin

Batter:

Shortening 1 cup
Sugar 2 cups
Eggs 4 large (or 5 medium)
"Adams® Best" Vanilla 2 teaspoons
Adams® Butter Flavoring 1 teaspoon
Flour 3 cups, sifted
Adams® Allspice 1 teaspoon
Adams® Cinnamon 1 1/2 teaspoon
Adams® Nutmeg 1/2 teaspoon
Salt 1/2 teaspoon
Baking soda 1 1/2 teaspoon
Buttermilk 3/4 cup
Apples 1 cup, fresh, finely chopped or grated
Pecans 1/2 cup, chopped

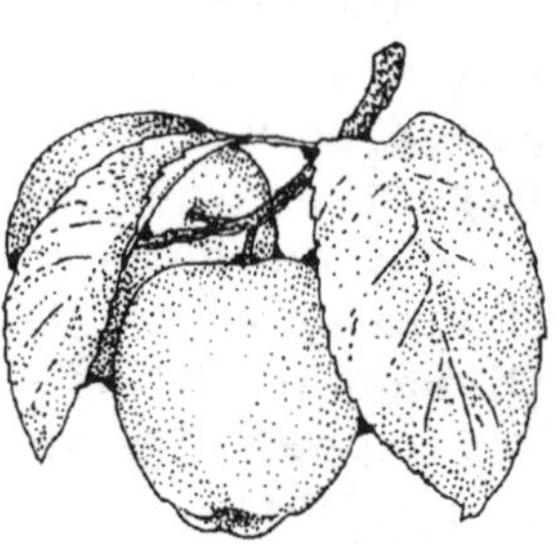

Preheat oven to 325 degrees. Batter: Cream shortening and sugar. Add eggs, one at a time. Add vanilla and butter flavoring. Mix well. Sift flour, allspice, cinnamon, nutmeg, salt, soda, then add alternately with buttermilk. Fold in apples and pecans. Blend well. Pour into a 10" stem or bundt pan that has been well greased and dusted with flour. Bake at 325 degrees for about 1 hour and 20 minutes, or until toothpick inserted into center comes out clean. Do not overbake. Remove cake from pan while still hot and brush on icing covering top and sides.

Icing:

Sugar 1 cup
Water 1/2 cup
Margarine 1 tablespoon
Apples 1/4 cup, fresh, crushed or grated
"Adams® Best" Vanilla 1/2 teaspoon
Adams® Butter Flavoring 1/2 teaspoon
Adams® Cinnamon 1/2 teaspoon

Combine all ingredients. Bring slowly to a boil, stirring constantly. Let boil 1 1/2 minutes, let sit for 2 minutes, then brush on hot cake.

Ice Box Fruit Cake

Beverly McClatchy - Midland

Graham crackers 1 pound, crushed
Marshmallows 1 pound
Milk 3/4 cup
Raisins 1 pound
Pecans 4 cups, chopped
Dates 1 package, chopped
Pineapple 1 small can, crushed
Maraschino cherries 1 small jar

Melt marshmallows and cracker crumbs in hot milk. Add fruit and nuts. Press into lightly greased casserole dish (oblong). Refrigerate and slice when cooled. Serves 10.

Sour Cream Pound Cake

Beverly McClatchy - Midland

Margarine 1 cup
Sugar 3 cups
Egg yolks 6
Vanilla 1 1/2 teaspoon
Flour 3 cups, sifted
Salt 1/2 teaspoon
Baking soda 1/4 teaspoon
Sour cream 1/2 pint
Egg whites 6, beaten

Cream margarine and sugar well (almost white). Add yolks individually. Add remaining ingredients (except egg whites) at once. Fold in beaten egg whites. Bake in greased and floured tube pan 300 degrees 1 1/2 hours. Serves 12-14.

Tip: Keep 1-2 cakes in the freezer for emergencies. Excellent served with fresh fruit.

East Texas Pecan Cake

Vernie Bailey - Kemp

Butter 2 cups
Flour 4 1/2 cups, sifted
Salt 1/8 teaspoon
Baking powder 1 teaspoon
Eggs 6
Brown sugar 1 pound
Milk 1/2 cup
Vanilla 1 teaspoon
Instant coffee 3 tablespoons
Pecans 4 cups, chopped

Set out butter to soften. Sift together flour, salt, baking powder. Grease bottom of 10 inch tube pan. Separate eggs; beat yolks well; beat egg whites until stiff. In a large mixing bowl, cream together butter and brown sugar. Add beaten egg yolks, mixing well. Combine milk, vanilla and coffee dissolved in 3 tablespoons hot water. Add alternately with dry ingredients. Fold in pecans and egg whites. Pour into pan and bake at 325 degrees 1 1/2 hours. Let cook in pan on cake rack. Remove from pan. Serves 12.

Prairie Beer Cake

Ola Marie Robison - Damon

Dates 2 cups, chopped
Pecans or other nuts 1 cup
Enriched all-purpose flour 3 cups, sifted (reserve 1/2 cup)
Butter or margarine 1 cup
Brown sugar 2 cups (1 lb.)
Eggs 2, well beaten
Salt 1/2 teaspoon
Baking soda 2 teaspoons
Cinnamon 1 teaspoon
Cloves 1/2 to 1 tablespoon
Beer 2 cups (any brand)

Grease and flour a 10 inch tube pan. Preheat oven to 350 degrees. Dredge dates and nuts in reserved flour. Cream butter and sugar. Add eggs and beat well. Sift dry ingredients together and add alternately with beer. Fold in dates and nuts. Bake at 350 degrees 1 hour in prepared pan. (You may also use bundt or angel food cake pan.) Keeps well. You can freeze all or a part of it for later use.

Buttermilk Carrot Cake

Nancy Plunk - Fort Worth

All-purpose flour 2 cups
Baking soda 2 teaspoons
Salt 1/2 teaspoon
Cinnamon 2 teaspoons
Eggs 3, well beaten
Vegetable oil 3/4 cup
Buttermilk 3/4 cup
Sugar 2 cups
Vanilla 2 teaspoons
Pineapple 1 (8 oz.) can, crushed
Carrots 2 cups, grated
Flaked coconut 1 (3 1/2 oz.) can
Nuts 1 cup, chopped

Combine flour, baking soda, salt, cinnamon and eggs; set aside. Combine oil, buttermilk, sugar, vanilla; beat until smooth. Stir flour mixture, pineapple, carrots, coconut and nuts into egg and oil mixture.

Pour batter into 2 greased and floured 9 inch round cake pans. Bake at 350 degrees for 35-40 minutes.

Immediately spread buttermilk mixture (see recipe below) evenly over layers. Cool in pans 15 minutes. Remove from pans and cool completely. Spread Orange-Cream Cheese Frosting (see recipe below) between layers and on top and sides of cake. Store in refrigerator.

Buttermilk Glaze:

Sugar 1 cup
Baking soda 1/2 teaspoon
Buttermilk 1/2 cup
Butter 1/2 cup
Light corn syrup 1 tablespoon
Vanilla 1 teaspoon

Combine all ingredients in pan except vanilla. Bring to a boil; cook 4 minutes stirring often. Remove from heat and stir in vanilla. Spread on hot cake layers.

Orange-cream Cheese Frosting:

Butter 1/2 cup, softened
Cream cheese 1 (8 oz.) package, softened
Vanilla 1 teaspoon
Powdered sugar 2 cups sifted
Grated orange rind 1 teaspoon
Orange juice 1 teaspoon

Combine butter and cream cheese, beat until fluffy. Add vanilla, sugar, rind and juice. Beat until smooth. Spread onto cooled cake. 10 servings.

Caramel Crater Cake

Florence E. Belzung - San Antonio

Yellow cake mix (1 package 2 layer size)
French Vanilla instant pudding mix 1 package (4 serving size)
All-purpose flour 1/2 cup
Vegetable oil 1/4 cup
Water 2/3 cup
Eggs 2
Vanilla extract 1 tablespoon
Butter flavoring 1 teaspoon
Dark brown sugar 1 cup, packed
Toasted walnuts or pecans 3/4 cup, chopped
Vanilla extract 2 teaspoons
Butter or margarine 1/4 cup, melted

Preheat oven to 350 degrees. Measure out 1 cup of dry cake mix; set aside for topping. Combine remaining cake mix, pudding mix, flour, oil, water, eggs, vanilla and butter flavorings. Beat at medium speed of mixer for 2 minutes. Pour into greased and floured 13 x 9 x 2 pan.

Topping:

Combine reserved 1 cup cake mix, brown sugar, walnuts or pecans and 2 teaspoons vanilla. Add melted margarine or butter. Mix until crumbly (actually this mixture is rather moist). Sprinkle on top of cake batter. Carefully cut through batter with knife to create marbled effect. Bake 30-35 minutes. Cool about 30 minutes before drizzling with glaze.

Glaze:

Powdered sugar 1 cup
Light corn syrup 1 tablespoon
Vanilla extract 1 tablespoon
Water 3 teaspoons

Combine all ingredients until smooth. Serves 18-24.

Apricot Surprise Coffee Cake

Carmen Dougherty - Marion

Apricots 1/2 cup, cut-up dried
Pineapple 1/2 cup, crushed, drained
Sugar 1/4 cup
Orange rind 1/4 teaspoon, grated
Orange juice 1 1/2 tablespoon
Coconut 1/3 cup, flaked
Flour 1 1/2 cups
Baking powder 2 teaspoons
Salt 3/4 teaspoon
Sugar 1/2 cup
Shortening 1/2 cup
Egg 1, well beaten
Milk 3/4 cup

Combine apricots, pineapple and 1/4 cup sugar. Cook and stir over low heat for 3 minutes or until fruit is clear. Cool. Add orange rind, juice and coconut. Measure sifted flour, add baking powder, salt and 1/2 cup sugar and sift again. Cut in shortening. Combine egg and milk, add to flour mixture and stir only until all flour is moist. Spread 2/3 of the batter in a greased 9 inch square pan. Alternate tablespoons of fruit mixture and remaining batter on top. Run spatula in a spiral through batter to give marbled effect. Bake at 400 degrees for 30 minutes. Serves 8.

Real Good Pecan Pie

Sunny Johnson - Streetman

Pie crust 9 inch
Eggs 3
Sugar 2/3 cup
Mrs. Butterworth's® Syrup 1 1/4 cups
Pecans 1 cup or more, coarsely chopped

Heat oven to 375 degrees. Beat all ingredients, except pecans with rotary beater. Mix in pecans. Pour into pastry-lined pie pan. Bake 40-50 minutes or until set and pastry nicely browned. Serve a la mode if desired. Serves 8.

Trinity River Mud Cake

Imperial Sugar Company - Sugar Land

Eggs 4
Sugar 2 cups
Butter or margarine 1 cup (2 sticks), melted
All-purpose flour 1 1/2 cups
Cocoa 1/3 cup
Vanilla 1 teaspoon
Shredded coconut 1 cup
Walnuts or pecans 2 cups, chopped (4 oz.)
Marshmallow cream 1 (7 oz.) jar

Combine eggs and sugar in mixer and mix at high speed for 5 minutes. Combine melted butter or margarine, flour, cocoa, vanilla, coconut and nuts. Combine the two mixtures and mix well. Bake in greased and floured 13 x 9 x 2 pan in preheated 350 degrees oven for 30 minutes or until cake tests done. For best results, bake on rack in middle of oven. Remove from oven and spread marshmallow cream over top of cake. Wait a few minutes, then frost while cake is still warm.

Floodtide Frosting:

Butter or margarine 1/2 cup (1 stick), melted
Milk 6 tablespoons
Cocoa 1/3 cup
Powdered sugar 1 pound (4 cups unsifted)
Vanilla 1 teaspoon
Walnuts or pecans 2 cups, chopped (4 oz.)

Combine all ingredients and mix well with wire whisk. Spread carefully over marshmallow cream.

Note: Cake is very rich and filling so it can be cut in small squares to feed a crowd.

German Chocolate Potato Cake

Imperial Sugar Company - Sugar Land

Moist, chocolate cake brings back memories of Grandma's baking.

Sugar 2 cups
Shortening 1 cup
Mashed potatoes 2 cups (without butter or other seasonings added)
Salt 1 teaspoon
Cloves 1 teaspoon
Cinnamon 2 teaspoons
Nutmeg 1 teaspoon
Eggs 4
Baking soda 2 teaspoons
Buttermilk 1 cup
Cocoa 1/2 cup
Flour 2 cups
Cooked raisins 2 cups
Nuts 1 cup, chopped

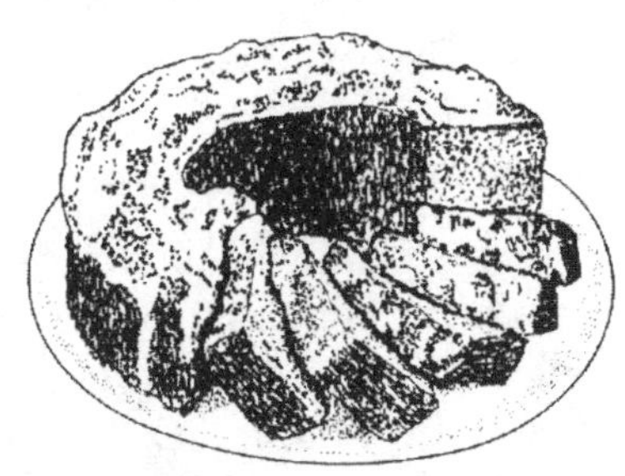

Preheat oven to 350 degrees. Lightly grease and flour large tube cake pan, large bundt pan or 12 x 8 x 2 loaf pan.

Cream together sugar, shortening, mashed potatoes, salt, cloves, cinnamon, nutmeg. Be sure all ingredients are thoroughly combined and free from lumps. Add eggs and beat thoroughly.

Combine soda and buttermilk and let stand a few minutes. Add cocoa and flour, sifted together, alternately with liquid to creamed mixture. Stir in cooked, thoroughly drained raisins and chopped nuts. Bake at 350 degrees for approximately 50-60 minutes, or until toothpick when inserted into center of cake comes out dry and cake is just beginning to pull away from pan. Do not overbake.

Guadalupe Mud Pie

Executive Chef John Billings, Y.O. Ranch Hilton - Kerrville

Oreo® cookies 1 package
Butter 1/4 pound
Blue Bell® vanilla ice cream 1/2 gallon
Bailey's® Irish Creme 1/4 cup
Kahlua® 1/4 cup
Pie shell
Hershey's® Fudge Topping 1 small can

Crush Oreo cookies in mixer. Melt butter. Add to crushed cookies and mix well. Pat mixture to 1/4 inch thickness into a 10 inch pie pan and freeze.

Mix ice cream with mixer until softened. Add liqueurs and mix until malt consistency. Pour into pie shell and freeze for 1 hour. Spread fudge topping evenly over top of ice cream mixture and freeze for 4 hours. Cut into 10 pieces.

Note: National Dairy Board 3rd Place Winner 1991

Simple Cheesecake

Mrs. Odie L. Crumby - Bonham

Graham cracker crumbs 1 1/4 cups
Sugar 1/4 cup
Crisco® 1/3 cup, melted
Cream cheese 2 (8 oz.), softened
Eagle Brand® sweetened condensed milk 1 (14 oz.) can
Eggs 3
Lemon juice 3 tablespoons
Sour cream 1 (8 oz.) container
Cherry pie filling 1 (21 oz.) can

Preheat oven to 300 degrees. Combine crumbs, sugar and shortening; press firmly on bottom of 9 inch springform pan. In another bowl beat cheese until fluffy. Gradually add condensed milk until smooth. Beat in eggs and lemon juice. Pour into prepared pan. Bake 45 minutes or until center is set. Top with sour cream, bake 5 minutes longer. Cool. Chill. Top with pie filling. If there are any leftovers, refrigerate. Serves 12-15.

Southern Burnt Cream Pie

Anelle Mack - Midland

Sugar 1 cup, divided
Water 1/2 cup, boiling
Flour 1/4 cup
Salt 1/8 teaspoon
Milk 1 1/2 cups
Egg yolks 2, beaten
Butter 1 1/2 tablespoon
Vanilla extract 1 teaspoon
Baked pie shell 1, 9 inch

Place 1/2 cup sugar in a heavy skillet and melt over medium heat until sugar turns to a light brown color. Stir in boiling water and boil mixture for 2 minutes.

Blend together remaining sugar, flour and salt. Add milk to sugar-flour mixture and mix until smooth. Stir in the burnt sugar syrup. Cook and stir over low heat until hot. Pour part of it over the beaten egg yolks. Then add yolks to hot mixture and cook until mixture coats a spoon. Add butter and vanilla. Cool filling. Fill pie shell.

Meringue:
Egg whites 2
Salt 1/8 teaspoon
Sugar 4 tablespoons

Beat together egg whites and salt until stiff. Gradually beat in the sugar. Put meringue on pie and bake at 300 degrees for 15-20 minutes. Serves 6.

Grandma's Old-Fashioned Peach Cobbler

Pat Stone - Conroe

Butter 1 stick, melted
Peaches 2 cans, extra large regular cling
Flour 1 cup
Sugar 1 cup
Milk 1 cup
Baking powder 2 teaspoons

Pour melted butter in 9 x 12 baking dish. Heat fruit on top of stove; sweeten if necessary. Combine remaining ingredients.

Pour flour mixture into melted butter in baking dish. Pour heated fruit into mixture in pan. Bake 35-40 minutes or until brown at 350 degrees. Serves 6.

Variation: Use fresh blackberries. Sweetened to taste and heated on top of stove.

Padre Island Sand Dollars

Imperial Sugar Company - Sugar Land

Butter 1 cup (2 sticks), softened
Powdered sugar 1/2 cup
All-purpose flour 2 cups
Vanilla 1 teaspoon
Salt 1/4 teaspoon
Sugar

Beat together butter and powdered sugar until creamy and fluffy. Gradually mix in flour. Stir in vanilla and salt and mix well. Using level tablespoonfuls of dough, shape into balls, press one side of each ball into sugar and place sugar sides up on ungreased cookie sheet. Cookies can be rather close together because they do not spread when cooking. Bake in preheated 400 degree oven about 10 minutes or until done but not browned. Remove from cookie sheets and cool completely on wire racks. 3 1/2 dozen cookies.

Texas Dewberry Cobbler

Mary Emma Wagnon - Seguin

Sugar 3/4 cup
Cornstarch 1 tablespoon
Water 1 cup, hot
Dewberries 3 1/2 cups
Vanilla 1 teaspoon
Butter 2 tablespoons
Cinnamon 1/2 teaspoon
Flour 1 cup
Sugar 1 tablespoon
Baking powder 1 1/2 teaspoons
Salt 1/2 teaspoon
Shortening 3 tablespoons
Milk 1/2 cup
Heavy cream (optional)

In sauce pan combine 3/4 cup sugar and cornstarch until well blended. Gradually add water and cook and stir until boiling, boil 1 minute. Add dewberries and vanilla. Pour into greased 1 1/2 quart casserole, dot with butter and sprinkle with cinnamon. In a bowl, combine flour, 1 tablespoon sugar, baking powder and salt. Cut in shortening to form fine particles. Add milk and stir just to blend. Drop by spoonfuls onto fruit mixture. Bake in preheated 400 degree oven for 30 minutes or until brown and bubbly. Serve warm; add cream if desired. Serves 4.

Chocolate Mousse

Wild Briar, the Country Inn at Edom - Ben Wheeler

Semi-sweet chocolate chips 12 ounces
Eggs 2 whole
Egg yolks 4
Egg whites 4
Vanilla 2 teaspoons
Heavy cream 2 cups
Powdered sugar 2 teaspoons

Melt chocolate chips. Separate 4 eggs into yolks and whites. Add 2 whole eggs to egg yolks. Beat and stir eggs into chips. Beat egg whites. Fold egg whites into chocolate mixture. Whip 3/4 cup of cream. Add 1 teaspoon vanilla. Fold into chocolate. Carefully pour into 12-14 of your prettiest champagne or wine glasses. Whip remainder of cream, add powdered sugar and vanilla as a topping when ready to serve. Makes 12-14 luncheon size or 6 dinner size servings.

Potato Chip Cookies

Wild Briar, the Country Inn at Edom - Ben Wheeler

Whipped margarine 1 pound tub
Sugar 1 1/2 cup
Flour 3 cups
Vanilla 2 teaspoons
Pecans 1 cup, chopped
Potato chips 1 cup, crushed

Cream margarine and sugar, add flour, vanilla, pecans and potato chips. Dough will be stiff. Drop by teaspoon on ungreased cookie sheet. Bake 15 minutes at 350 degrees. Freezes well.

The Big Cookie

Vernie Bailey - Kemp

Soft butter 1/2 cup
Sugar 1/4 cup
Light brown sugar 1/4 cup
Cocoa 1 tablespoon
Egg 1, well beaten
Vanilla 1/2 teaspoon
Flour 1 1/2 cups, sifted
Baking soda 1/2 teaspoon
Salt 1/2 teaspoon
Nuts 1/2 cup, chopped
Chocolate pieces 1 cup, chopped

Cream butter, sugars and cocoa. Add egg and vanilla. Combine flour, baking soda and salt; add to mixture. Fold in nuts and chocolate pieces. Drop by tablespoons onto greased baking sheet. Bake in preheated oven at 375-400 degrees for 12-14 minutes. Cool on wire rack. 24 cookies.

Four Layered Delight

Pat Stone - Conroe

First layer:

Flour 2 cups
Pecans or walnuts 1 cup, chopped
Margarine 2 sticks, melted

Mix ingredients together, press into 9 x 13 pan. Bake for 10-15 minutes at 425 degrees. Cool thoroughly.

Second layer:

Cream cheese 1 (8 oz.) package
Cool Whip® 2 1/2 cups
Powdered sugar 1 1/2 cup

Blend ingredients with mixer until creamy. Spread on first layer.

Third layer:

Instant pudding 2 small packages (any flavor)

Mix pudding as directed. Spread on second layer.

Fourth layer:

Cool Whip® 2 - 2 1/2 cups
Pecan sprinkles

Spread Cool Whip over third layer. Sprinkle with pecans.

Refrigerate. 8-10 servings.

Pecan trees grow everywhere in Texas. They are raised commercially in the Rio Grande Valley and in the state's midlands. Pecan, from the Algonquian word meaning "a hard-shelled nut" (although there are also soft-shelled varieties), is a truly American native product.

Pretzel Salad Dessert

Adele Tibbs - Big Spring

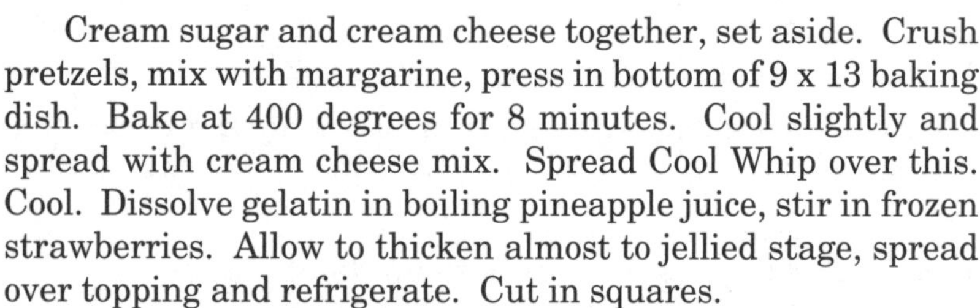

Sugar 1 1/2 cups
Cream cheese 12 ounces
Pretzels 3 cups, crushed
Margarine 1 stick
Cool Whip® 1 large
Strawberry gelatin 6 ounce package
Pineapple juice 2 cups
Strawberries 1 large package, frozen

Cream sugar and cream cheese together, set aside. Crush pretzels, mix with margarine, press in bottom of 9 x 13 baking dish. Bake at 400 degrees for 8 minutes. Cool slightly and spread with cream cheese mix. Spread Cool Whip over this. Cool. Dissolve gelatin in boiling pineapple juice, stir in frozen strawberries. Allow to thicken almost to jellied stage, spread over topping and refrigerate. Cut in squares.

Spanish Flan

Anelle Mack - Midland

Sugar 1/2 cup
Sweetened condensed milk 1 2/3 cup
Milk 1 cup
Eggs 3
Egg yolks 3
Vanilla 1 teaspoon
Whipped cream
Slivered almonds 1 cup coarsely chopped, toasted

Sprinkle sugar evenly in 9 inch cake pan; place over medium heat. Caramelize until lightly brown; cool. Combine remaining ingredients (except whipped cream and almonds) in blender; blend at high speed for 15 seconds. Pour over caramel mixture; cover with foil and place in large shallow pan with 1 inch water. Bake 350 degrees for 55 minutes. Invert onto serving plate. Serve with whipped cream and toasted almonds. Serves 6-8.

Rice Festival Pudding

Imperial Sugar Company - Sugar Land

A dessert recipe very popular with visitors to the annual rice festivals at Bay City and Winnie.

Long grain rice 1/2 cup
Water 1 cup
Salt 1/2 teaspoon
Milk 1 quart
Butter or margarine 1/2 stick
Eggs 3, beaten
Sugar 1/2 cup
Seedless raisins 1 cup
Vanilla 1/2 teaspoon

Add rice and salt to boiling water in a large sauce pan. Cover and cook over low heat 7-10 minutes, or until water is absorbed. Add milk and butter or margarine, stir and bring to boil. Turn heat to very low and when milk has ceased boiling (to prevent boiling over), cover and cook for about 1 hour, or until milk is almost absorbed. Add sugar, raisins and vanilla to beaten eggs. Pour into the rice, stirring slowly until rice begins to thicken. May be served hot, warm or cold. Serves 4-6.

Brown Sugar Bread Pudding

Adele Tibbs - Big Spring

Bread cubes 2 cups
Brown sugar 1/2 cup
Salt 1/4 teaspoon
Cinnamon 1 teaspoon
Vanilla 1 teaspoon
Milk 2 1/2 cups
Raisins 1/2 cup
Eggs 2, slightly beaten
Walnuts 1/2 cup, chopped
Butter 2 teaspoons

Combine bread cubes with brown sugar, salt and cinnamon. Add vanilla, milk, raisins, eggs and walnuts. Pour mixture into well-greased 1 quart baking dish. Dot with butter. Bake at 325 degrees for 45 minutes or until knife inserted in pudding comes out clean.

Pride House Poached Pears in Cream and Praline Sauces

Pride House Bed & Breakfast, Ruthmary Jordan - Jefferson

Pear 1 per serving **Praline sauce** **Creme fraiche**

Using hard preserving pear, not eating pears, core and peel the desired number of pears. In a large sauce pan cover the pears with water and poach over very low heat until done, 30 minutes or more (depending on size of pears). Refrigerate pears until ready to use. Drain the pears on a clean sponge. While the pears are on the sponge, puncture the bottom one-third of each fruit several times all the way through with an ice pick. This will keep the pear upright and also prevent it from rising above the bottom.

Praline Sauce

Brown sugar 1 box
Water 1 cup, cold
Karo® syrup 1/2 cup
Vanilla (Mexican is best)

Creme Fraiche

Combine:
Sour cream 24 ounces
Heavy whipping cream 3 pints
Powdered sugar 3/4 cup

In a saucepan bring brown sugar, water and syrup to a slow boil. Remove from heat just before liquid starts to sheet. Add vanilla to taste. Cool and store in refrigerator until ready to use.

To assemble, pour three or four tablespoons of praline sauce into the bottom of a tavern glass or other large clear container. Place the pear on top of the praline sauce in the glass. Carefully pour the creme fraiche into the glass until the creme line is a little over halfway up the pear. A clean line should remain between the two sauces for a dramatic presentation.

The innkeeper at Pride House takes pride in her cooking. The establishment in Jefferson, Texas claims to be the first bed-and-breakfast in Texas. After growing up on a Louisiana plantation, teaching school in Houston and operating two restaurants in Jefferson, Ruthmary Jordan accepted the innkeeper position at Pride House.

Strawberry Pizza

JoAnn Tucker - Chico

Crust:

Margarine 1 stick, soft
Flour 1 cup
Confectioner sugar 1/4 cup

Mix crust and pat in pizza pan. Bake at 350 degrees until slightly brown about 10-12 minutes.

Filling:

Sweetened condensed milk 1 can
Lemon juice 1/3 cup
Vanilla 1 teaspoon
Cream cheese 8 ounces, softened

Cream and spread over cooled crust.

Glaze:

Sugar 1 cup
Water 1 cup
Cornstarch 2 tablespoons
Strawberry gelatin 3 tablespoons
Red food color few drops

Cook until thick and cool. Spread on top of filling.

Topping:

Strawberries 2 pints, sliced on top of glaze
Whipped cream or Cool Whip®

Sprinkle with sliced strawberries and top with whipped cream.

Refrigerate. Serves 10-12.

Log Nut Roll

Ola Marie Robison - Damon

Marshmallow cream 1 (7 oz.) jar
Vanilla 1 teaspoon
Powdered sugar 1 pound, sifted
Candy caramels 1 1/2 pounds
Pecans 9 1/2 cups, chopped

Combine marshmallow cream and vanilla. Gradually sift powdered sugar into marshmallow cream and vanilla mixture. Knead the dough until smooth. Divide the marshmallow dough into 12 equal parts, roll into logs about 3/4 inch in diameter. Place on wax paper-lined cookie sheet and freeze for at least 3 hours. Melt caramels in double boiler, then dip frozen candy in caramel and immediately drop into pan of pecans, pressing nuts into caramel being careful not to get sticky caramel on hands. Store in covered container. Slice and enjoy.

Dishpan Cookies

Llano Grande Plantation Bed & Breakfast - Nacogdoches

So called because it requires a large pan to mix its 17 cups of ingredients!

Sugar 1 3/4 cups
Brown sugar 2 1/4 cups
Oil 2 cups
Eggs 4
Vanilla 2 teaspoons
Baking soda 2 teaspoons
Flour 4 cups
Salt 3/4 teaspoon
Raisins or dates 1 1/4 cup, chopped
Nuts 1 cup, chopped
Oatmeal 1 1/2 cup, raw
Cornflakes 3 3/4 cups, slightly crushed

Dump in pan and mix. Better if refrigerated a few hours. Drop by spoonful on ungreased cookie sheet. Bake at 350 degrees 10-12 minutes until brown. Makes a great number of cookies but they disappear quickly and they freeze well, if some are left over.

Nut Roll

Ethel Jean Wells - Arlington

Graham crackers 1 pound, rolled fine to crumbs
Marshmallow tidbits 1 pound
Dates 1 cup, chopped
Cream 1/4 cup or half & half
Maraschino cherries red or green 1 small jar
Pecans 2 cups, chopped, or black or English walnuts
Figs 1 cup, chopped (optional)

Mix graham cracker crumbs with the marshmallow tidbits and dates. Knead lightly together. Add 1/8 cup of half & half or cream, be sure only enough to moisten mixture. Add cherries, chopped nutmeats and figs (optional), kneading very thoroughly in a large pan or bowl. Slowly add remainder of cream only as you knead and knead very well until mixture all holds together. Then form mixture in 2 large rolls and roll each in aluminum foil. Place in freezer. Do not attempt to slice before 24 hours. This is very rich and a dollop of whipped cream may be added to each slice. May be kept for 6 months in freezer.

Note: I keep this for church groups or bridge clubs because one can cut according to size of group. Very nice for holidays. When cutting, since it is frozen, I run my large butcher knife under hot water to slice easily.

Gast Haus Pudding

Gast Haus Lodge Bed and Breakfast - Comfort

Bread 10-12 cups, cut into 2 x 2 inch pieces
Milk 5 cups
Eggs 4, whole large
Granulated sugar 3/4 cup
Vanilla 2 tablespoons
Apple pie seasoning 1 teaspoon
Cinnamon 1 teaspoon, ground
Raisins 3/4 cup
Cinnamon 'n Spice apple filling and topping 1 can (21 oz.)
Egg whites 4, stiffly beaten
Margarine or butter 1 stick, melted
Lemon sauce (recipe below)

In large bowl, mix bread pieces with milk. Stir to coat, allowing bread to absorb milk.

In separate bowl, combine whole eggs, sugar, vanilla, apple pie seasoning, cinnamon, raisins and pie filling. Add to bread mixture. Stir until blended. Fold in beaten egg whites and melted butter. Mix to combine. Pour in greased 9 x 13 inch baking pan. Place pan in larger pan. Pour hot water 1 inch deep into larger pan. Bake in 350-degree oven 45 to 55 minutes or until center appears set and firm. Serve warm topped with warm lemon sauce.

Lemon Sauce:

Granulated sugar 2/3 cup
Cornstarch 2 tablespoons
Water 2 cups
Butter or margarine 6 tablespoons
Lemon juice 3 tablespoons, fresh
Salt pinch

In double boiler, combine sugar and cornstarch. Add water. Cook over medium heat, stirring constantly, until mixture thickens. Remove from heat. Add butter or margarine, lemon juice and salt.

Honey Peanut Butter Balls

Milk 1 cup, nonfat dry
Peanut butter 1 cup
Honey 1 cup
Vanilla 1/2 teaspoon
Peanuts 2/3 cup, chopped
Wheat germ 1 cup

Mix well, roll into 1 inch balls and refrigerate. Makes about 4 dozen.

Chewy Chocolate-Peanut Clusters

Peanut butter 2 tablespoons
Butterscotch morsels 16-ounce package
Semisweet chocolate morsels 6-ounce package
Peanuts 2 cups, roasted Spanish

Combine peanut butter, butterscotch morsels and chocolate morsels in a heavy saucepan; cook over low heat, stirring constantly until melted. Stir in peanuts. Drop by rounded teaspoonfuls onto wax paper; chill until firm. Store in an airtight container in refrigerator. Makes about 4 dozen.

The Best Peanut Brittle

Bonnie Dixon - Alvarado

Sugar 3 cups
Light corn syrup 1 cup
Water 1/2 cup
Peanuts 3 cups, raw
Margarine 1 tablespoon
Salt 1 teaspoon
Baking soda 2 teaspoon

Boil sugar, syrup and water to medium ball (240 degrees) on candy thermometer. Add peanuts and stir until temperature reaches hard crack (300 degrees). Remove from heat, add margarine, salt and soda. Immediately pour in large buttered metal tray (cookie sheet) or platter. Cool and break into pieces.

Tip: Store in airtight container.

Texas Punch

Orange juice concentrate 12-ounce can, frozen
Lemonade concentrate 6-ounce can, frozen
Limeade concentrate 6-ounce can, frozen
Cranberry juice concentrate 6-ounce can, frozen
Pineapple juice 46-ounce can
Peach or apricot nectar 46-ounce can
Ice
Citrus slices

Dilute frozen juices with water according to directions. Mix with pineapple juice and nectar. Pour over ice in a large punch bowl. Garnish with citrus slices.

Rum Eggnog

Eggs 4
Sweetened condensed milk 14-ounce can
Rum 1/2 cup
Cinnamon 1/2 teaspoon
Vanilla extract 1 teaspoon
Ground nutmeg

In a blender, mix all of the ingredients except nutmeg. Serve in small glasses. Sprinkle with touch of ground nutmeg. Serves 6.

Margaritas

Lime 1, halved
Salt
Ice
Tequila 2/3 cup
Triple Sec or Grand Marnier 1/3 cup
Lime juice 2/3 cup
Limeade 2/3 cup
Sugar 3 teaspoons
Lime wedges

Freeze stemmed glasses. Rub cut lime around the rim of glass and dip in a dish containing salt. In a blender, combine ice, Tequila, Triple Sec, lime juice, limeade and sugar. Blend until ice is thoroughly crushed. For frothy margarita, blend on high speed. Serve in salt-rimmed glasses. Garnish with lime wedges.

Note: For strawberry margaritas, add sliced strawberries to mix before blending and garnish with a sugar-dipped strawberry.

Banana Pineapple Smoothie

Banana 1
Pineapple juice 1 1/2 cups
Ice cubes 4

Mix ingredients in blender until ice is thoroughly crushed. Serve immediately.

Note: For an "instant breakfast," add an egg and a little milk to the mixture before blending.

Hot Mocha

Milk 2 cups
Instant chocolate 2 teaspoons
Instant coffee 2 teaspoons

Heat milk in a saucepan over a low heat. Stir in chocolate and coffee until thoroughly combined. Serve in mugs. A dollop of whipped cream and a sprinkle of cinnamon makes it extra special. Serves 2.

Index

P—S

T—Z

Cook Books from Golden West Publishers

CHRISTMAS IN TEXAS

Recipes, traditions and folklore for the Holiday Season — or for all year long! Create southwestern holiday spirit with this wonderful cook book!

5 1/2 x 8 1/2 — 128 pages . . . $8.95

SALSA LOVERS COOK BOOK

More than 180 taste-tempting recipes for salsas that will make every meal a special event! Salsas for salads, appetizers, main dishes, and, even, desserts! Put some salsa in your life! By S. K. Bollin.

5 1/2 x 8 1/2—128 pages . . . $5.95

CHILI-LOVERS COOK BOOK

Chili cookoff prize-winning recipes and regional favorites! The best of chili cookery, from mild to fiery, with and without beans. Plus a variety of taste-tempting foods made with chile peppers. 200,000 copies in print! By Al and Mildred Fischer.

5 1/2 x 8 1/2—128 pages . . . $5.95

THE TEQUILA COOK BOOK

Taste the spirit and flavor of the Southwest! More than 150 recipes featuring tequila as an ingredient. Wonderful appetizers, soups, salads, main dishes, breads, desserts and drinks. Includes fascinating trivia. Truly a unique cook book. By Lynn Nusom.

5 1/2 x 8 1/2—128 pages . . . $7.95

WHOLLY FRIJOLES!

The Whole Bean Cook Book

Features a wide variety of recipes for salads, main dishes, side dishes and desserts with an emphasis on Southwestern style. Recipes for pinto, kidney, garbanzo, black, red and navy beans, and many more! Includes cooking tips and fascinating bean trivia! By Shayne Fischer.

5 1/2 x 8 1/2—112 pages . . . $6.95

ORDER BLANK

GOLDEN WEST PUBLISHERS

4113 N. Longview Ave. • Phoenix, AZ 85014

602-265-4392 • **1-800-658-5830** • FAX 602-279-6901

Qty	Title	Price	Amount
	Arizona Cook Book	**5.95**	
	Best Barbecue Recipes	**5.95**	
	California Country Cook Book	**6.95**	
	Chili-Lovers' Cook Book	**5.95**	
	Christmas in New Mexico Cook Book	**8.95**	
	Christmas in Texas Cook Bok	**8.95**	
	Colorado Favorites Cook Book	**5.95**	
	Cowboy Cartoon Cook Book	**5.95**	
	Easy Recipes for Wild Game & Fish	**6.95**	
	Joy of Muffins	**5.95**	
	Mexican Desserts & Drinks	**6.95**	
	Mexican Family Favorites Cook Book	**6.95**	
	New Mexico Cook Book	**5.95**	
	Pecan-Lovers' Cook Book	**6.95**	
	Quick-n-Easy Mexican Recipes	**5.95**	
	Real New Mexico Chile Cook Book	**6.95**	
	Salsa Lovers Cook Book	**5.95**	
	Tequila Cook Book	**7.95**	
	Texas Cook Book	**5.95**	
	Wholly Frijoles! The Whole Bean Cook Book	**6.95**	

Shipping & Handling Add ➡	U.S. & Canada Other countries	$2.00 $5.00	

☐ My Check or Money Order Enclosed $

☐ MasterCard ☐ VISA ($20 credit card minimum)

(Payable in U.S. funds)

Acct. No. Exp. Date

Signature

Name Telephone

Address

City/State/Zip

2/96 **Call for FREE catalog** TEXAS CB

This order blank may be photo-copied.